Progressive PIANO METHOD

Book Two

By Andrew Scott and Gary Turner

Acknowledgements
Cover photo by Phil Martin
Instruments supplied by Allans Music
Special thanks to Philip Peddler

Distributed by

AUSTRALIA
Koala Publications Pty. Ltd.
37 Orsmond Street,
Hindmarsh 5007
South Australia
Ph: (08) 346 5366
Fax: 61-8-340 9040

USA
Koala Publications Inc.
3001 Redhill Ave.
Bldg 2#109
Costa Mesa
CA. 92626
Ph: (714) 546 2743
Fax: 1-714-546 2749

U.K. and Europe
Music Exchange,
Mail Order Dept,
Claverton Rd, Wythenshawe,
Manchester M23 9ZA
Ph: (0161) 946 1234
Fax: (0161) 946 1195

Order Code KP-PM2

ISBN 1 875726 27 6

Please leave in Stud. piano

Contents

Introduction .... **page 5**

Lesson 1 .... **page 6**
The D Chord 6
My Bonnie Lies Over the Ocean 6

Lesson 2 .... **page 8**
The Note C♯
(in the third space of the treble staff) 8
The D Major Scale 8
The Note C♯
(in the second space of the bass staff) 9
The A7 Chord 9
The Key of D Major 10
Row, Row, Row Your Boat 10

Lesson 3 .... **page 11**
The G Chord (2nd Inversion) 11
The Daring Young Man
on the Flying Trapeze 12

Lesson 4 .... **page 13**
The Natural Sign 13
Take Me Out to the Ball Game 14

Lesson 5 .... **page 16**
12 Bar Blues 16
12 Bar Blues in the Key of C 16
The Note A (above the treble staff) 17
12 Bar Blues in the Key of G 18
The Note E♭
(in the 4th space of the treble staff) 19
12 Bar Blues in F 19

Lesson 6 .... **page 20**
The Note G♯ (below Middle C) 20
The E7 Chord 20
Minor Chords 21
The Am Chord 21
Harem Dance 22

Lesson 7 .... **page 23**
Minor Scales 23
The A Natural Minor Scale 23
Minor Keys 23
Minor Key Signatures 24
E Natural Minor Scale 25
The Em Chord 25

Lesson 8 .... **page 26**
The Note D♯ (below Middle C) 26
The B7 Chord 26
The Harmonic Minor Scale 27
The Note G♯ (above the treble staff) 27
The A Harmonic Minor Scale 27

Lesson 9 .... **page 28**
The Note D♯
(on the 4th line of the treble staff) 28
Enharmonic Notes 28
E Harmonic Minor Scale 29
Minka 29
Em Key Signature 29

Lesson 10 .... **page 30**
The Dm Chord 30
The D Natural Minor Scale 31
The D Harmonic Minor Scale 31
Dm Key Signature 31
Modulation 32
We Three Kings of Orient Are 32

Lesson 11 .... **page 34**
Am Chord (2nd Inversion) 34
When Johnny Comes Marching Home 34

Lesson 12 .... **page 36**
Dm Chord (2nd Inversion) 36
The Volga Boatman 36
Em Chord (1st Inversion) 37
Turnaround Progressions 37
English Country Gardens 38

Lesson 13 .... **page 39**
Syncopation 39
Strike up the Band 39
Under the Bamboo Tree 40

Lesson 14 .... **page 41**
The Sixteenth Note 41
Arkansas Traveller 42

Lesson 15 .... **page 43**
The Dotted Eighth Note 43
Funeral March 43
C Chord (1st Inversion) 44
Dm Chord (1st Inversion) 44
The Eighth Rest 45
The 1812 Overture 45
G7 Chord (another hand position) 46
Here Comes the Bride 46

Lesson 16 .... **page 47**
The 6/8 Time Signature 47
Slow Tempo 6/8 47
The Pleasure of Love 48
Fast Tempo 6/8 49
The Irish Washerwoman 49
Mexican Hat Dance 50

Lesson 17 .... **page 51**
The Note C♯ (next to Middle C) 51
Mexican Dance 51
The A7 chord (another hand position) 52
Lavender's Blue 53

Lesson 18 .... **page 54**
The Note G♯
(on the 2nd line of the treble staff) 54
El Condor Pasa 54

Lesson 19 .... **page 56**
The Note D♯ (below the treble staff) 56
Creepy Blues 56

Lesson 20 .... **page 58**
The Cut Time Signature 58
Hello My Baby 59

Lesson 21 .... **page 60**
The Triplet 60
Amazing Grace 61

Lesson 22 .... **page 62**
Swing Rhythms 62
By the Light of the Silvery Moon 63

Lesson 23 .... **page 64**
More Enharmonic Notes 64
The Chromatic Scale 64
Minuet in G 65

Lesson 24 .... **page 66**
The F♯ Diminished Chord 66
Ballin' the Jack 67
The Entertainer 68

Lesson 25 .... **page 70**
The G Augmented Chord 70
Mary's a Grand Old Name 71

Major Chord Chart 72
Minor Chord Chart 73
Seventh Chord Chart 74
Minor Seventh Chord Chart 75
Augmented Chord Chart 76
Diminished Chord Chart 76

Introduction

Progressive Piano Method, consisting of two books, has been designed to introduce the basics of playing piano and reading music to the student who has no previous musical knowledge. All the songs have been carefully graded into an easy-to-follow, lesson-by-lesson format.

To maximise enjoyment and interest, each book contains an extensive repertoire of well known songs with easy arrangements, playing basic chord shapes with the left hand, and melodies with the right hand.

Method Book 1 introduces the student to playing and reading music in the keys of C, F and G major over a range of more than two octaves. It gives basic left hand chord shapes and inversions for C, F, G7, B♭, C7, G and D7. These chords are combined with right hand melodies in 4/4 and 3/4 time, incorporating whole, half, quarter, eighth and dotted notes, with their equivalent rests. The C, F and G major scales are also introduced, along with sharp and flat notes.

At the completion of this book, the student will be able to play over 50 songs. The book also has a chord chart section listing basic shapes for all major, minor and seventh chords.

Method Book 2 extends the playing and reading to include the keys of D major, A minor, E minor and D minor, and expands the range of notes to include all chromatic notes. It introduces the following new chords – D, A7, E7, Am, Em, Dm, B7, diminished and augmented chords. Cut time, 6/8 time, syncopation and swing rhythms are also explained, along with sixteenth notes, dotted eighth notes and triplets. Natural and harmonic scales, as well as the chromatic scale are also covered.

At the completion of this book the student will be able to play an additional 30 songs, along with 12 bar blues and turnaround progressions.

The chord chart section at the end of the book is expanded to include minor seventh, augmented and diminished shapes.

Lesson 1

The D Chord

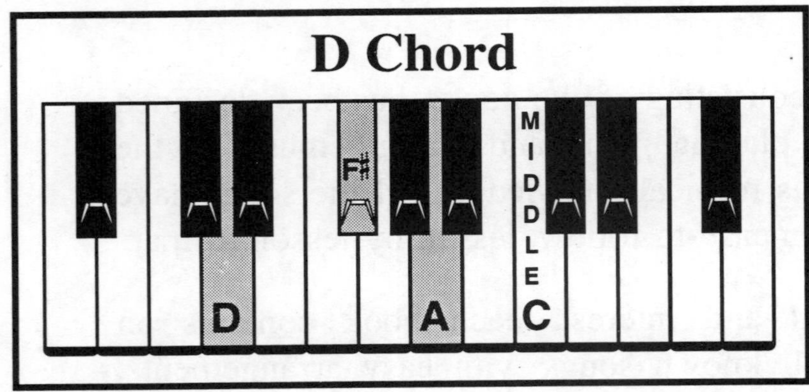

To play the D chord, use the **first**, **third** and **fifth** fingers of your **left** hand, as shown in the D chord diagram.

Exercise 1

2. My Bonnie Lies Over the Ocean

Traditional

On the recording there are **five** beats to introduce this song.

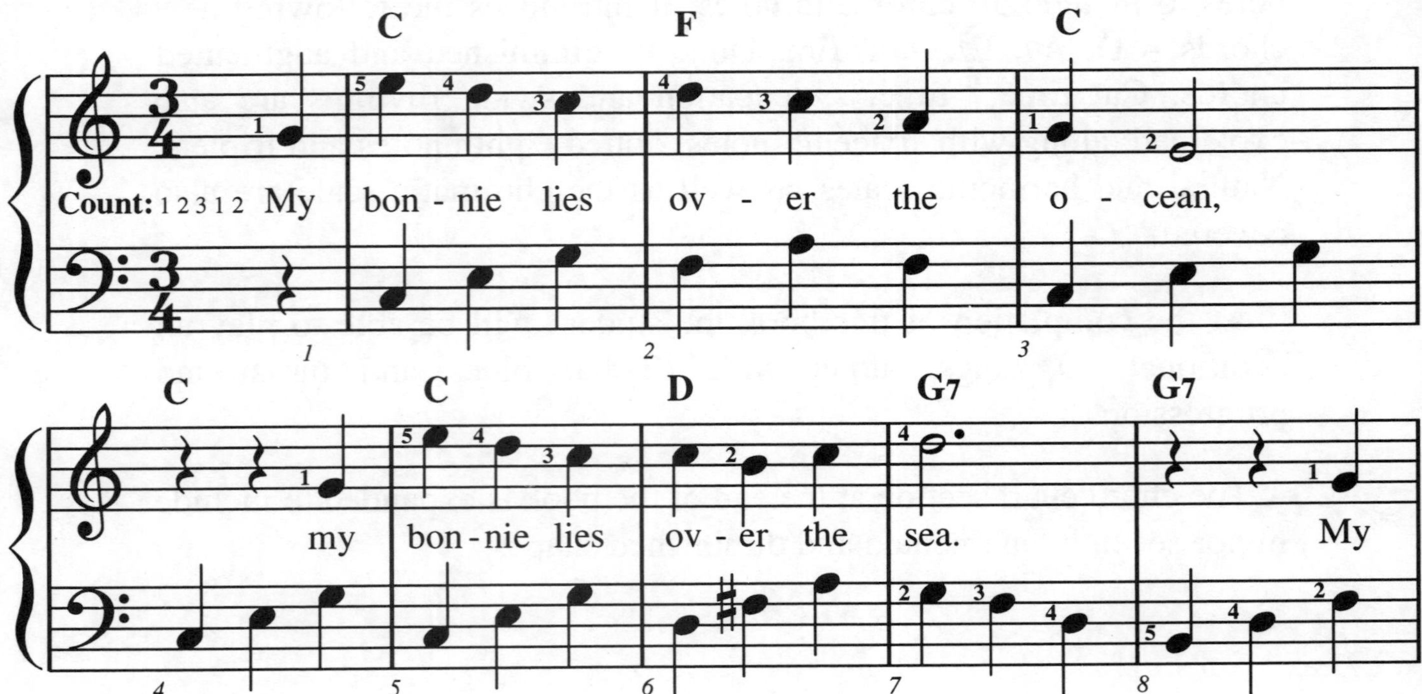

C F C C D
bon-nie lies ov - er the o-cean, so bring back my
9 10 11 12 13

G7 C C C C
bon-nie to me. Bring back,
14 15 16 17 18

F F G7 C C
Bring back, bring back, bring back my bon - nie to
19 20 21 22 23

C C C F F
me, Bring back, bring back, O
24 25 26 27 28

G7 G7 C C
bring back my bon - nie to me ______.
29 30 31 32

Lesson 2

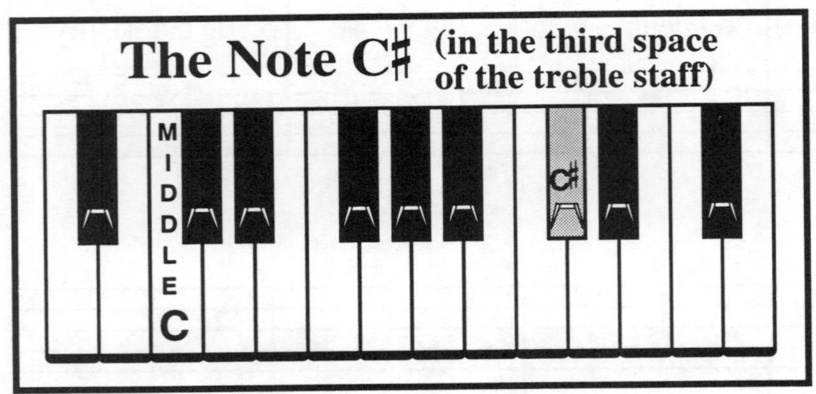

The Note C♯
(in the third space of the treble staff)

The C♯ note is the black key immediately to the right of the C note as shown in the diagram.

3. The D Major Scale

You now know enough notes to play the D major scale. The D major scale begins and ends on a D note and contains two sharps – F♯ and C♯.

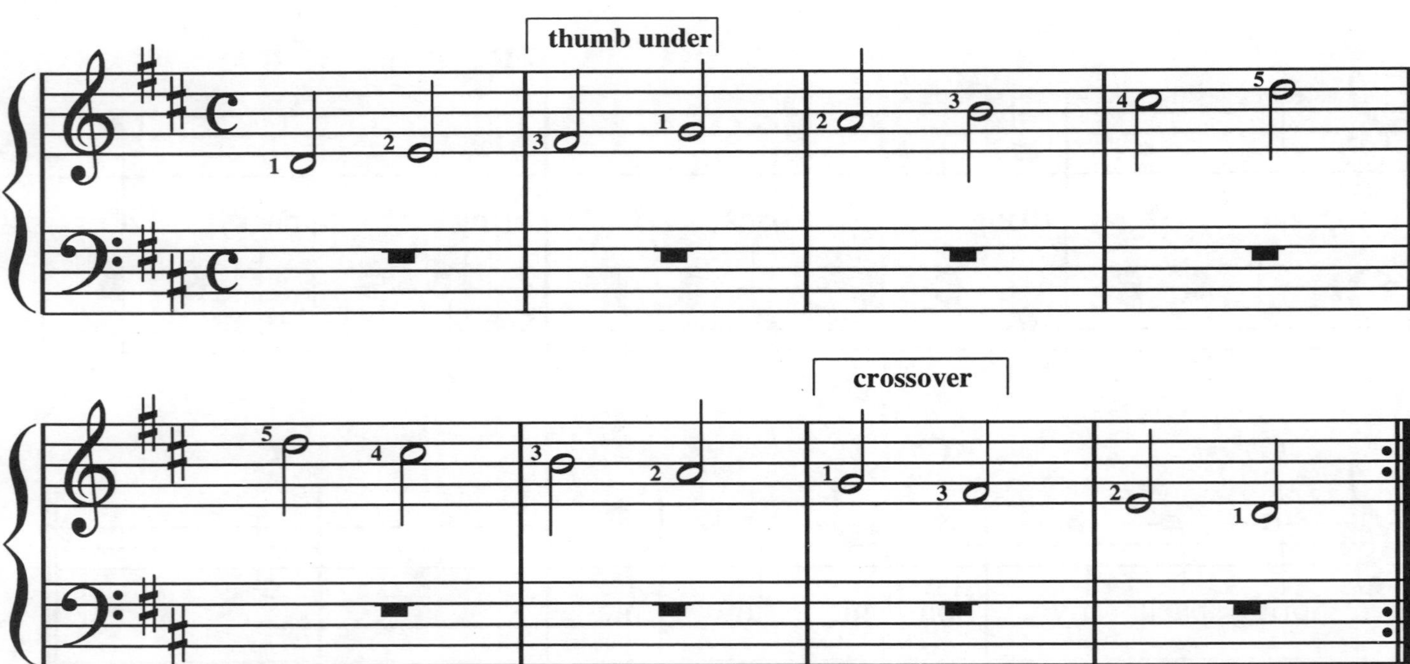

The ♯ signs after the clefs indicate that all F and C notes on the stave are played as F sharp and C sharp respectively.

The Note C♯
(in the second space of the bass staff)

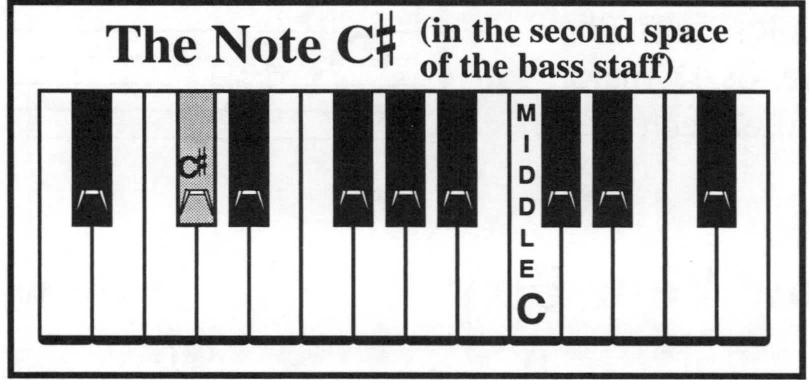

The note C♯, is the black key immediately to the right of the C note as shown in the diagram.

The A7 Chord

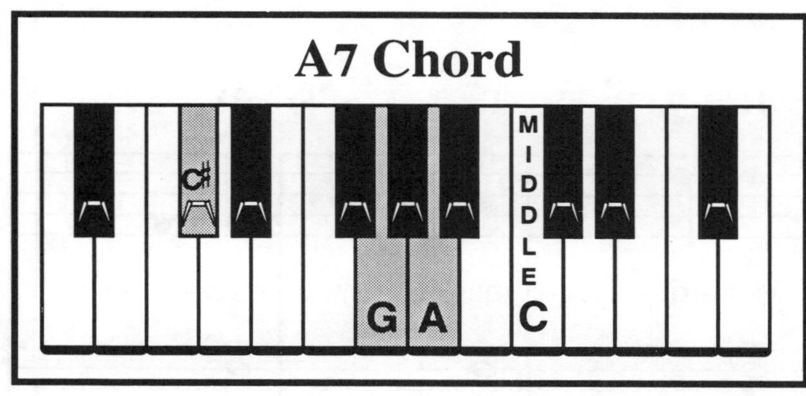

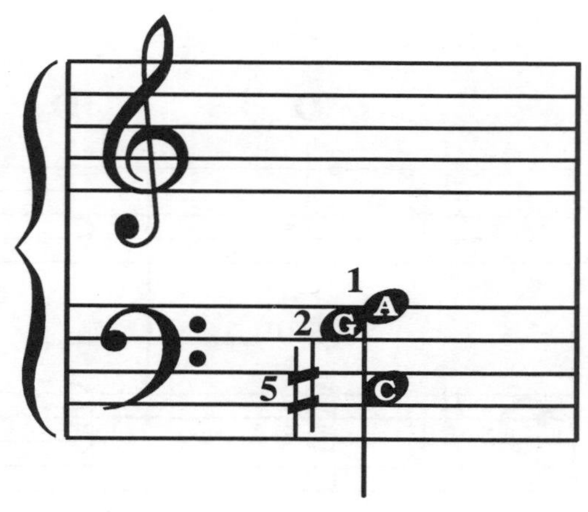

To play the A7 chord use the **first**, **second** and **fifth** fingers of your **left** hand.

Exercise 4

The Key of D Major

The song Row, Row, Row Your Boat is in the key of D major and contains notes from the D major scale. The key signature of D major contains two sharps (F♯ and C♯) after each clef.

5. Row, Row, Row Your Boat

Traditional

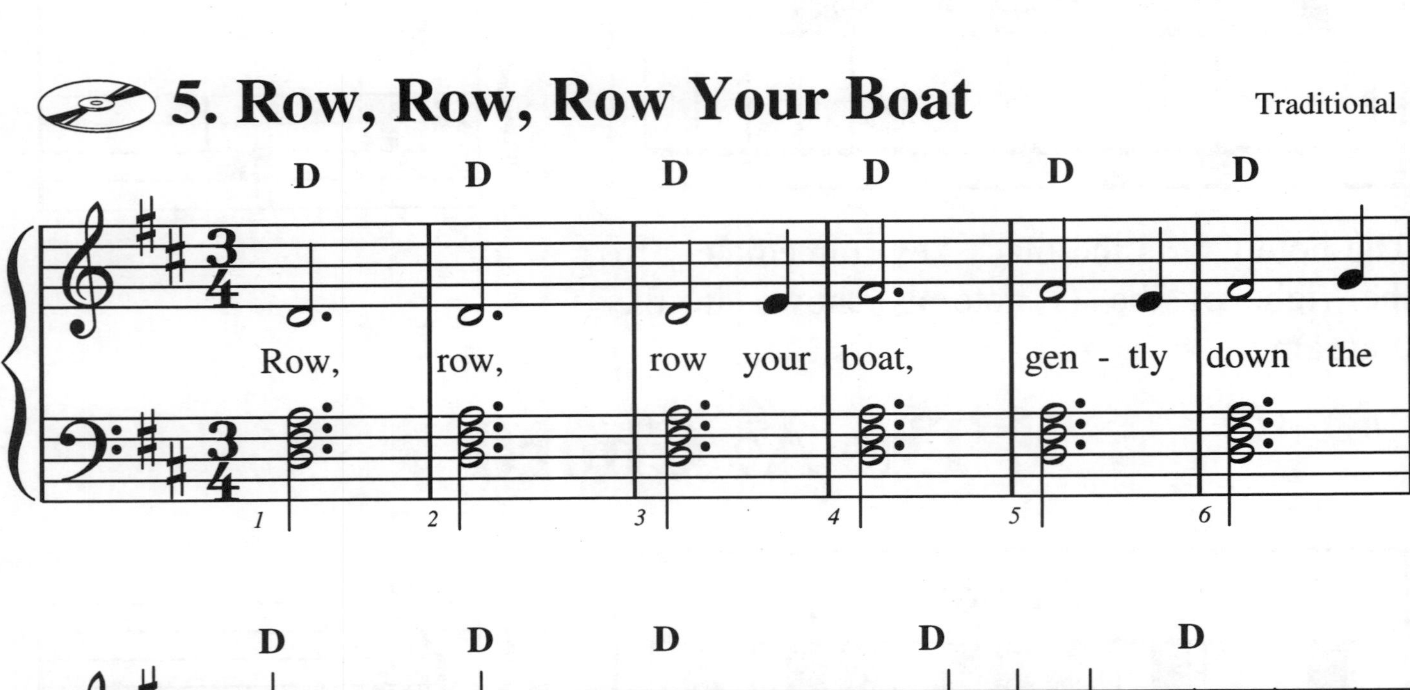

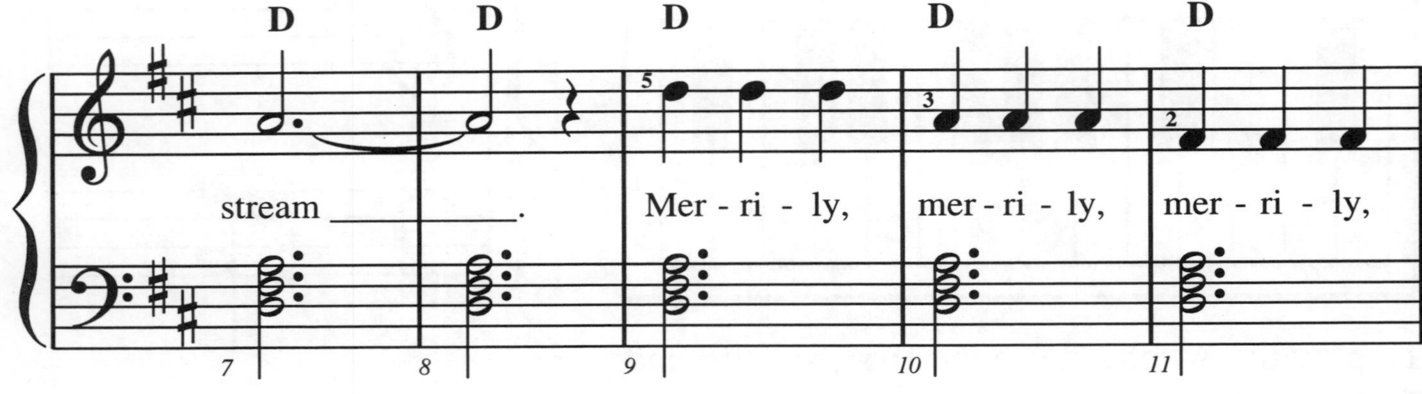

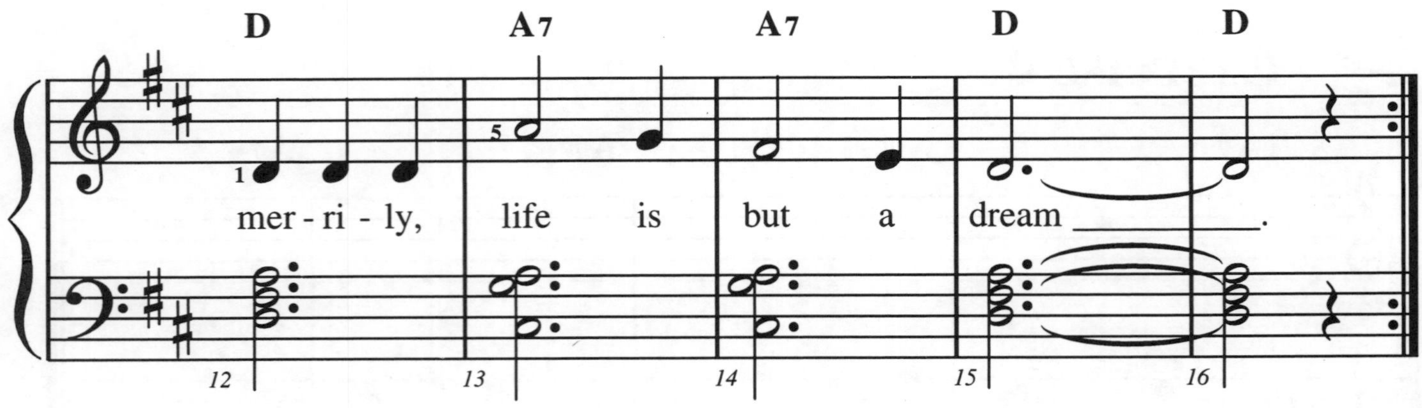

Lesson 3

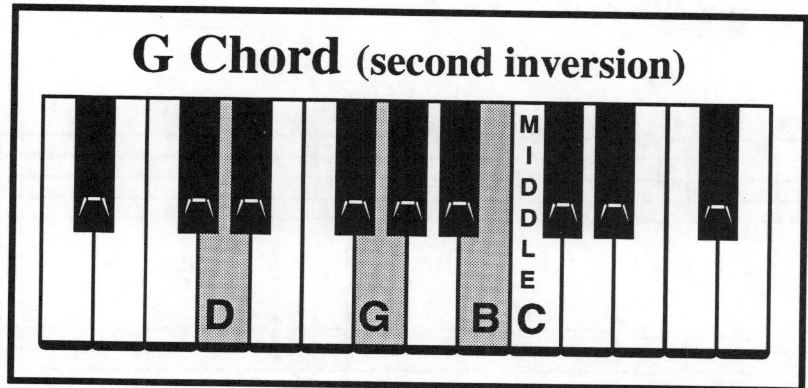

The G Chord

(second inversion)

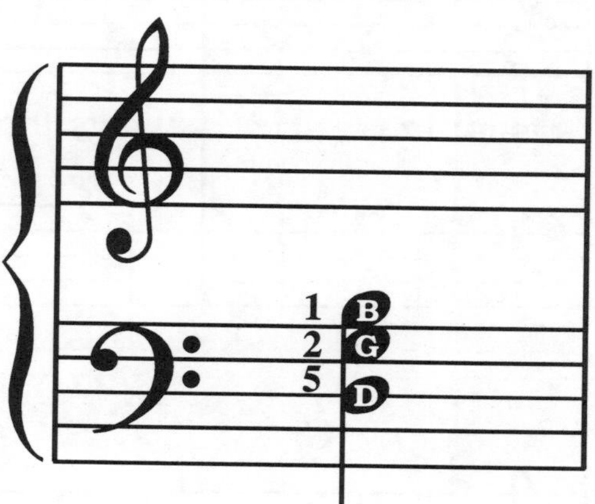

To play this G chord use the **first**, **second** and **fifth** fingers of your **left** hand. The G chord in this diagram is a second inversion of the G chord you learnt on page 56 of Book One.

Exercise 6

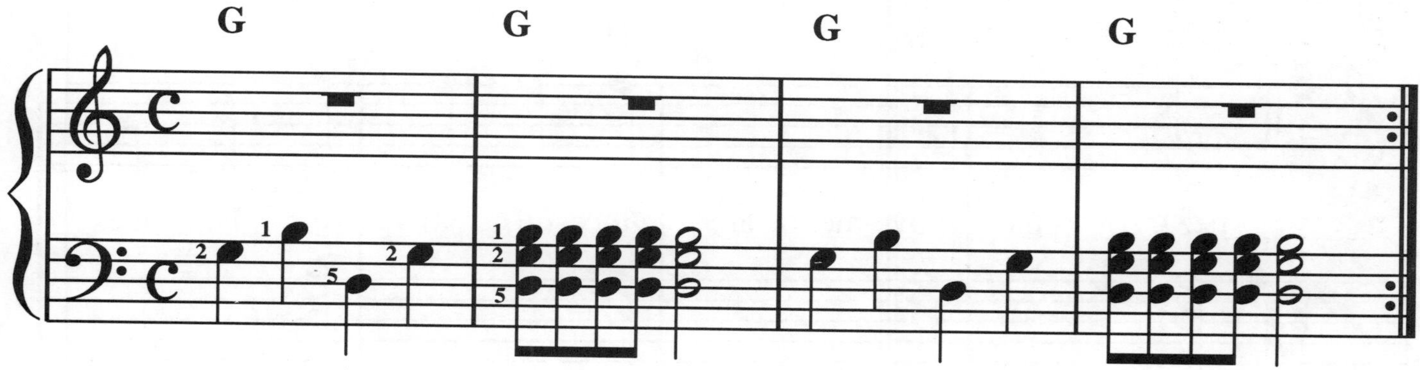

Exercise 7

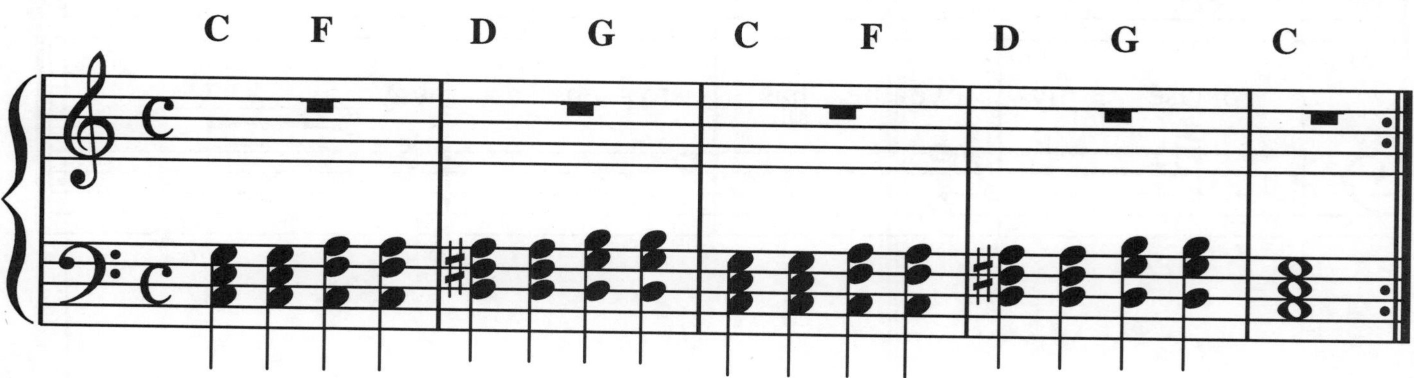

8. The Daring Young Man on the Flying Trapeze

Traditional

On the recording there are **five** beats to introduce this song.

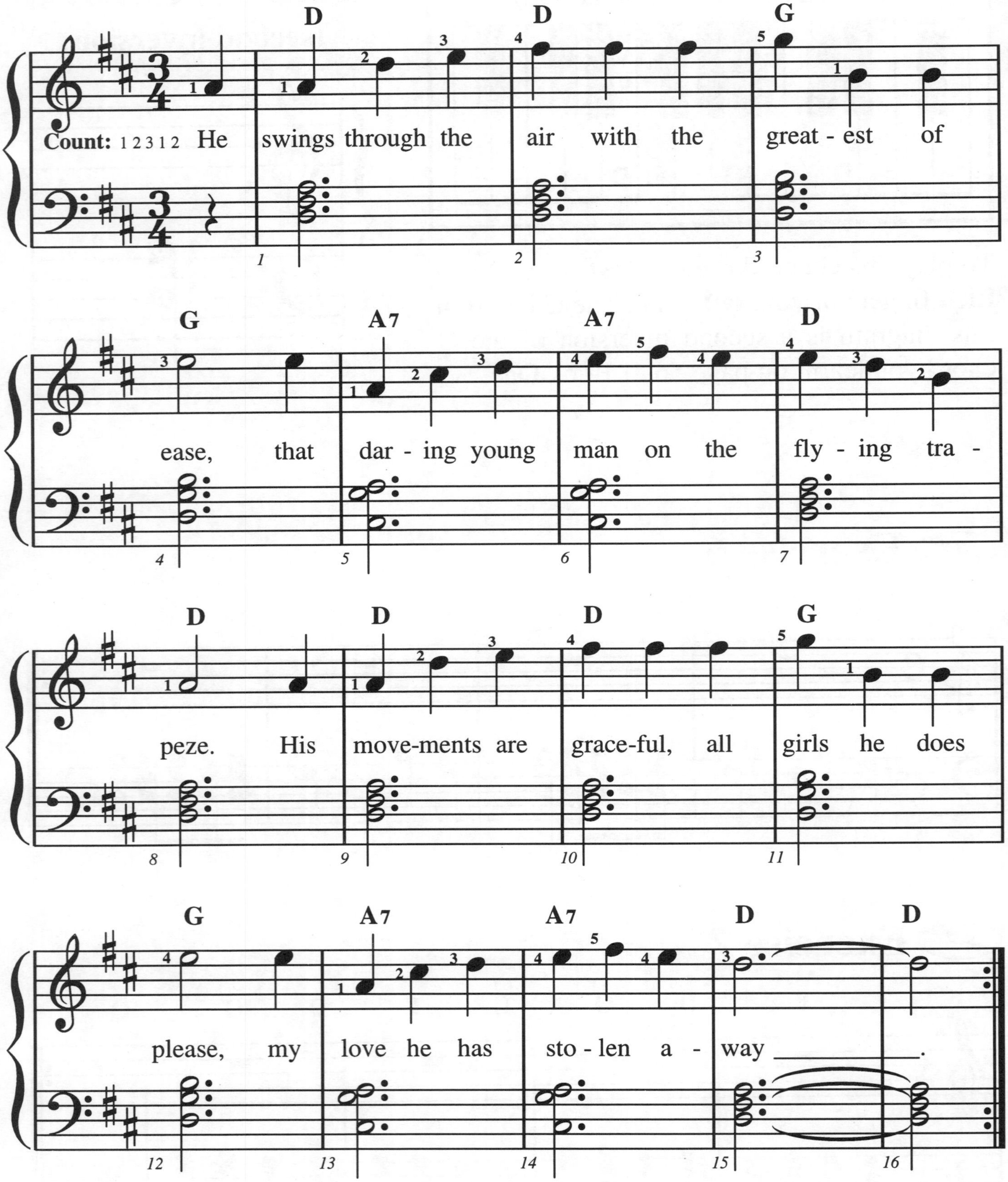

He swings through the air with the great - est of

ease, that dar - ing young man on the fly - ing tra -

peze. His move-ments are grace-ful, all girls he does

please, my love he has sto - len a - way ___________.

Lesson 4

The Natural Sign

This is a **natural** sign.

A natural sign cancels the effect of a sharp or flat. E.g., in bars 1, 2 and 3 of Exercise 9 there is a natural sign before the second to last note. The natural sign cancels the effect of the flat sign before the first B note (which would otherwise apply for the whole bar), and means that you play the third B note as B instead of B♭.

Exercise 9

Exercise 10

11. Take Me Out to the Ball Game

Jack Norworth and
Albert von Titzer

F
F
C7
C7
root, root, root for the home team, If
17
18
19
20
F
F
B♭
B♭
they don't win, it's a shame ______, For it's
21
22
23
24
B♭
B♭
F
F
one, two, three strikes, you're out, At the
25
26
27
28
G
C7
F
F
old ball game.
29
30
31
32

Lesson 5
12 Bar Blues

12 Bar Blues is a pattern of 3 chords which repeats every 12 bars. There are hundreds of well-known songs based on this chord progression, i.e., they contain basically the same chords in the same order. 12 bar blues is commonly used in rock music.

Some well known songs which use this 12 bar chord pattern are:

Batman TV Theme
Hound Dog – Elvis Presley
Rock Around the Clock – Bill Haley
Roll Over Beethoven – Chuck Berry
Blue Suede Shoes – Elvis Presley
In the Mood – Glenn Miller
Good Golly Miss Molly – Little Richard
Shake, Rattle and Roll – Bill Haley
Barbara Ann – The Beach Boys
Johnny B Good – Chuck Berry
Dizzy Miss Lizzy – The Beatles

Play the following 12 bar blues which is in the key of C major, and uses the C, F and G7 chords. When a song is said to be in the key of C major, it means that the most important chord (and usually the first chord) is the C chord.

This pattern of chords will probably sound familiar to you.

12. 12 Bar Blues in the Key of C

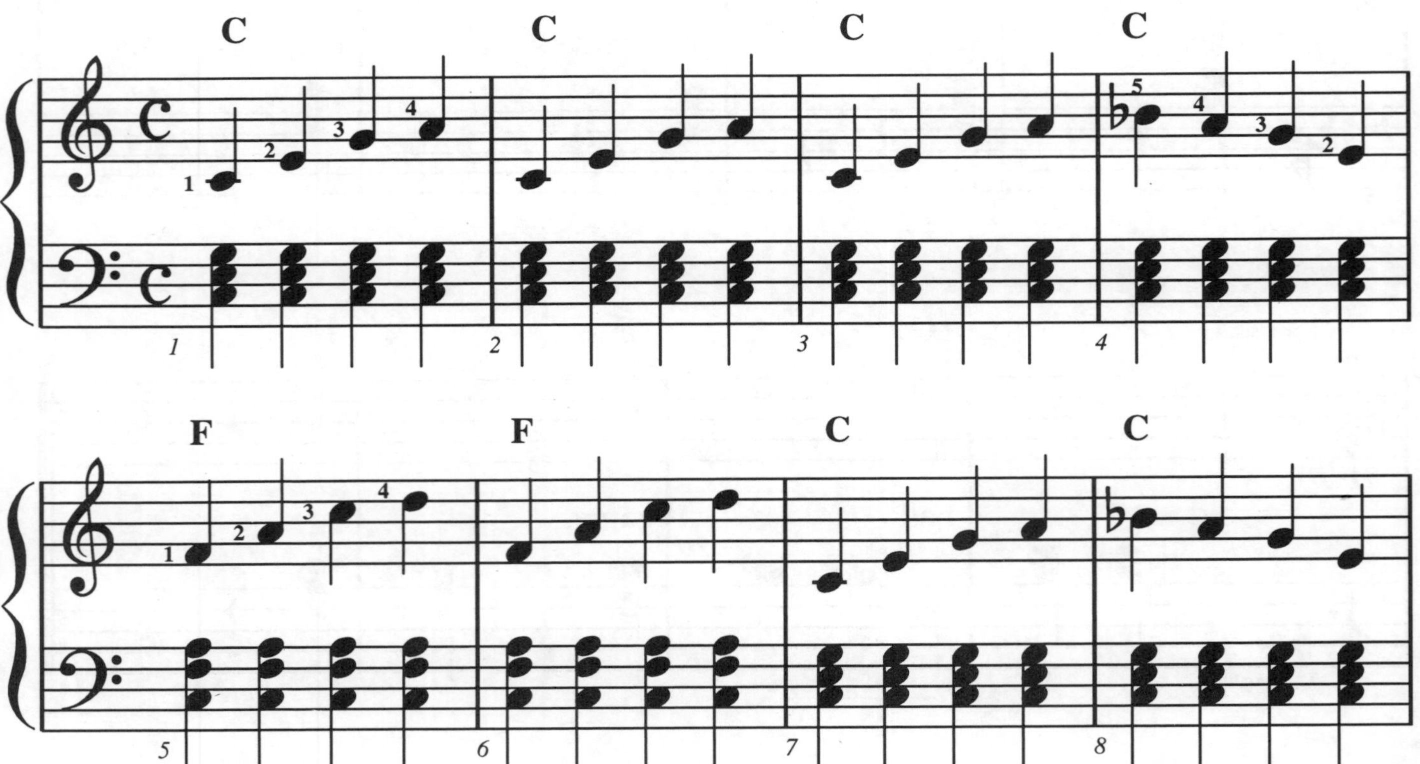

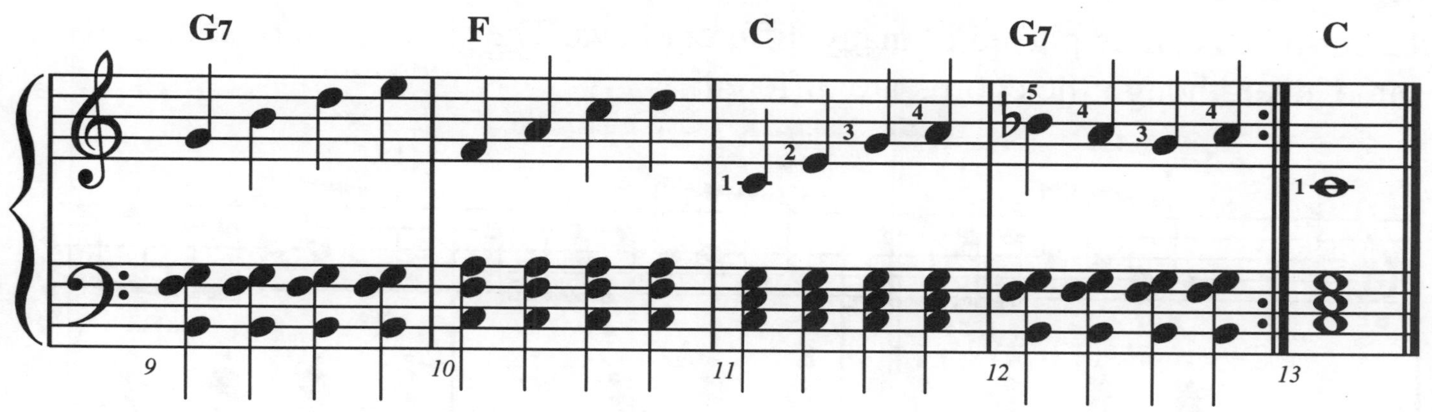

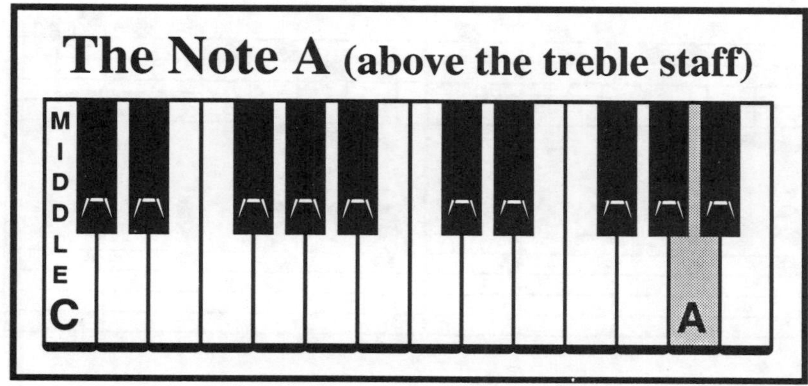

The Note A

(above the treble staff)

In this lesson, play the A note with the **fifth** finger of your **right** hand.

Exercise 13

14. 12 Bar Blues in the Key of G

12 bar blues can be played in many different keys. The chord pattern sounds the same, even though the chords are different.

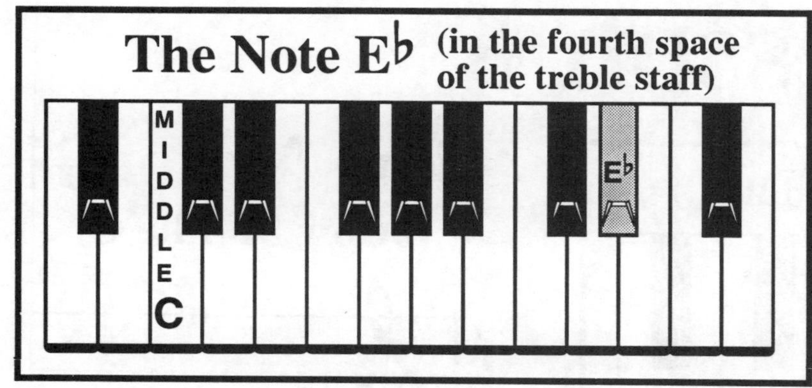

The Note E♭
(in the fourth space of the treble staff)

The note E♭ is the black key immediately to the left of the E note as shown in the diagram.

15. 12 Bar Blues in F

Practise the right hand carefully in this blues and observe the fingering method.

Lesson 6

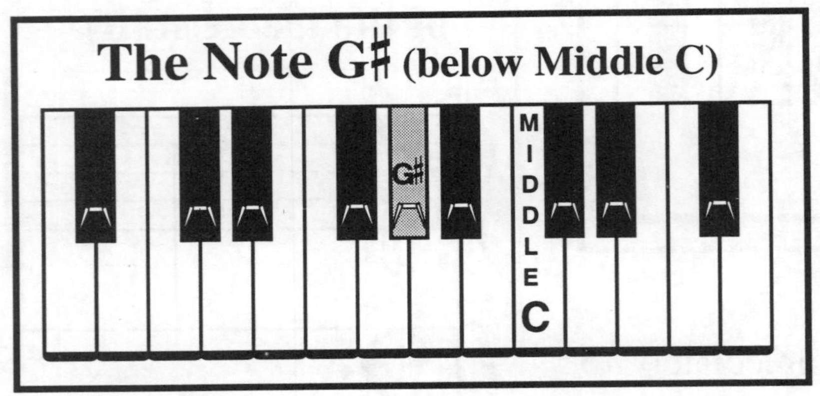

The Note G♯ (below Middle C)

The G♯ note is the black key immediately to the right of the G note as shown in the diagram.

The E7 Chord

The E7 chord contains the G♯ note given above. To play the E7 chord, use the **first**, **second** and **fifth** fingers of your **left** hand, as shown in the E7 chord diagram.

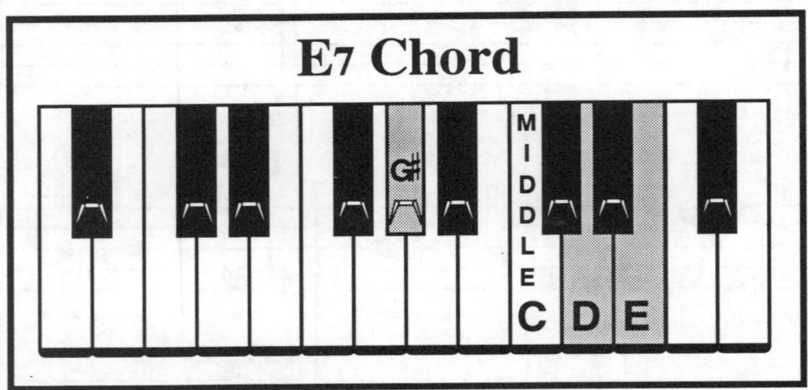

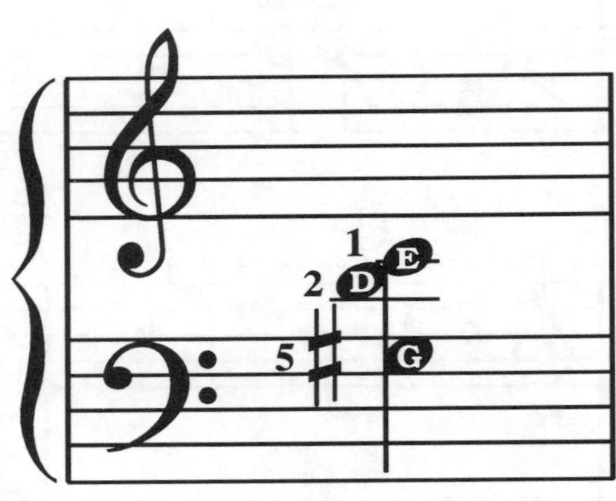

Exercise 16

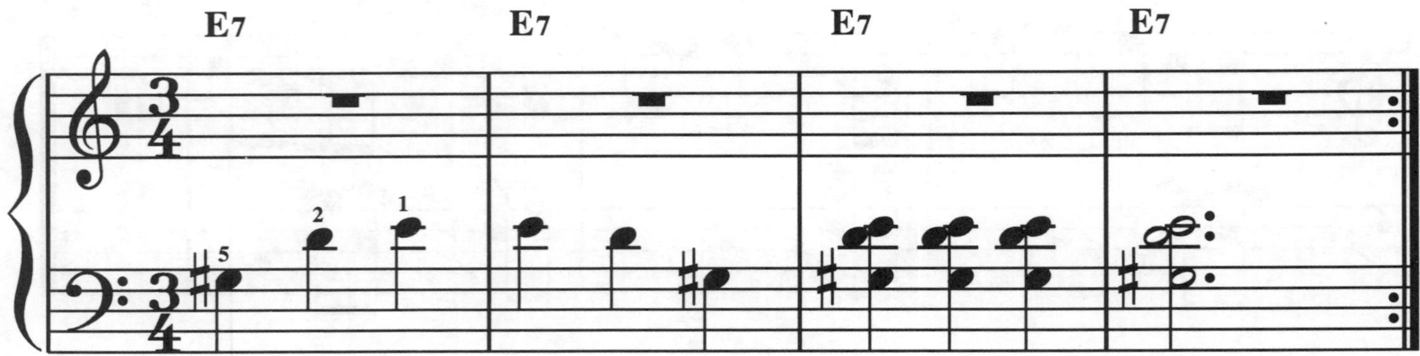

Exercise 17

Minor Chords

There are three main types of chords: major, seventh and minor chords. You have already learnt some major chords and some seventh chords. The first minor chord you will learn is the A minor chord. A minor chord is indicated by a small "m" written after the chord name, e.g. Am.

The A minor (Am) Chord

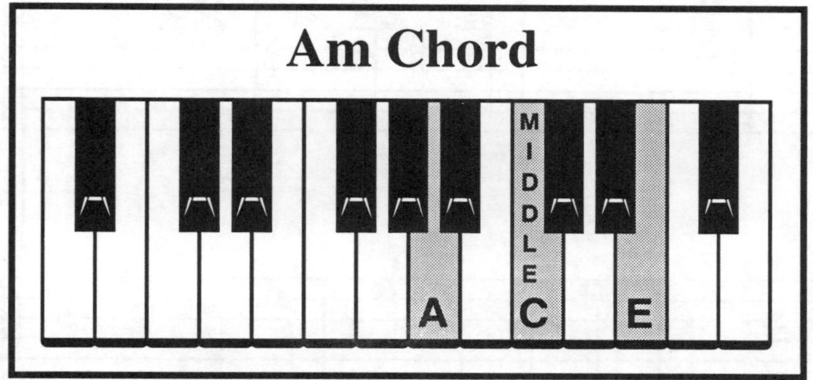

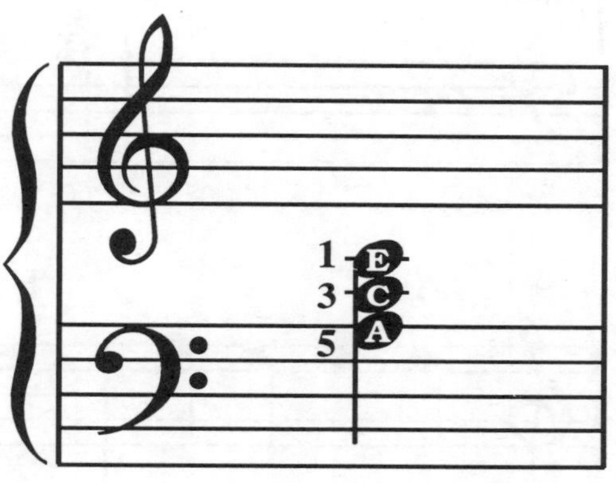

To play the Am chord use the **first**, **third** and **fifth** fingers of your **left** hand as shown in the diagram.

Exercise 18

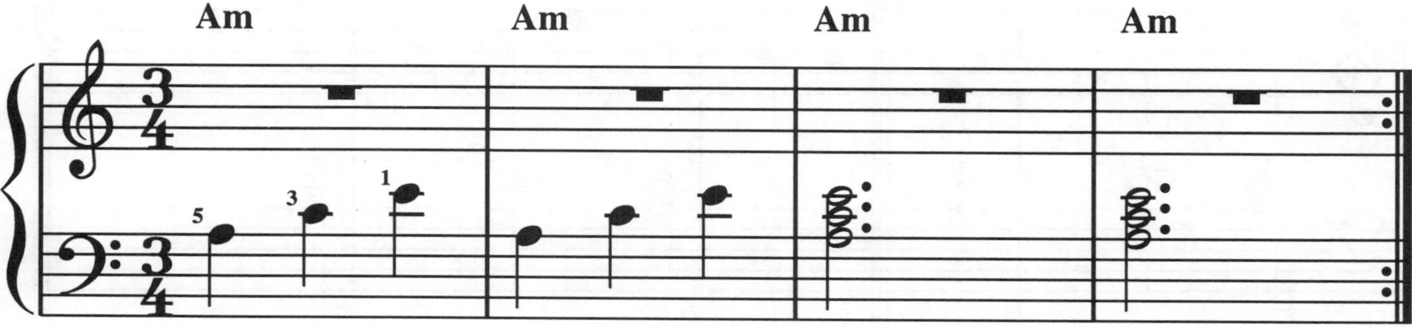

Exercise 19

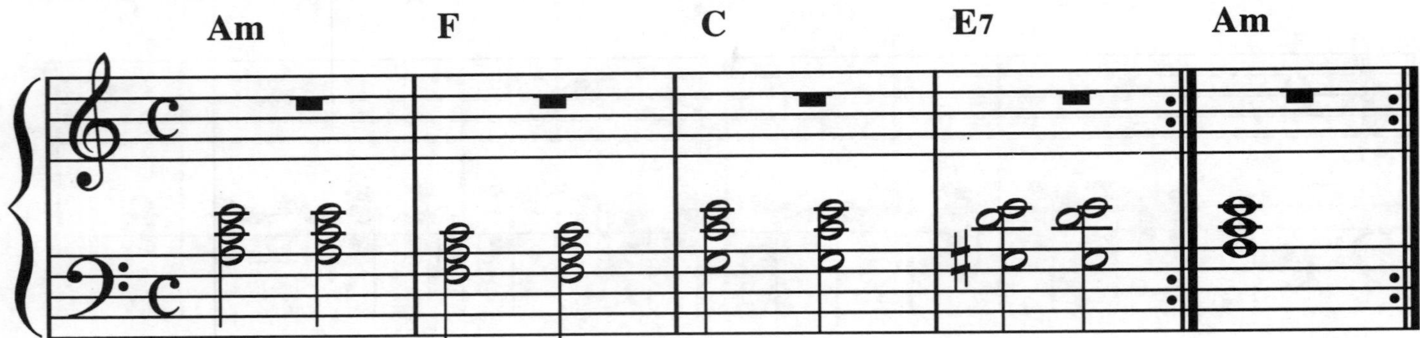

20. Harem Dance

Traditional

On the recording there are **six** beats to introduce this song.

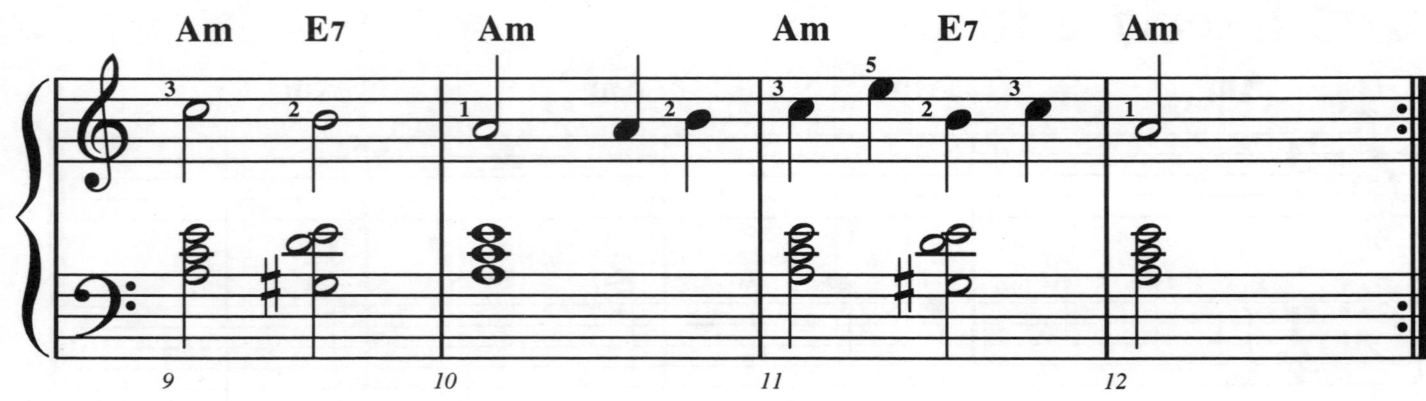

Lesson 7

Minor Scales

There are several different kinds of minor scales. The first minor scale you will study is called the natural minor scale.

21. The A Natural Minor Scale

Relative Scales

If you compare the A natural minor scale with the C major scale you will notice that they contain the same notes (except they start on a different note). Because of this, these two scales are referred to as being "**relative**": A minor is the "relative minor" of C major, and C major is the "relative major" of A minor.

Minor Keys

Whereas a melody written in a major key uses notes from the major scale, songs in a minor key use notes from the minor scale. The song Harem Dance on the previous page is in the key of Am because it uses notes from the A natural minor scale.

Key Signatures

Here is a summary of the key signatures you have studied so far.

The above key signatures are for major keys.

Minor Key Signatures

Relative majors and minors have the same key signature, e.g. Am is the relative minor of C major and contains no sharps or flats. So the key signature of Am is the same as C major.

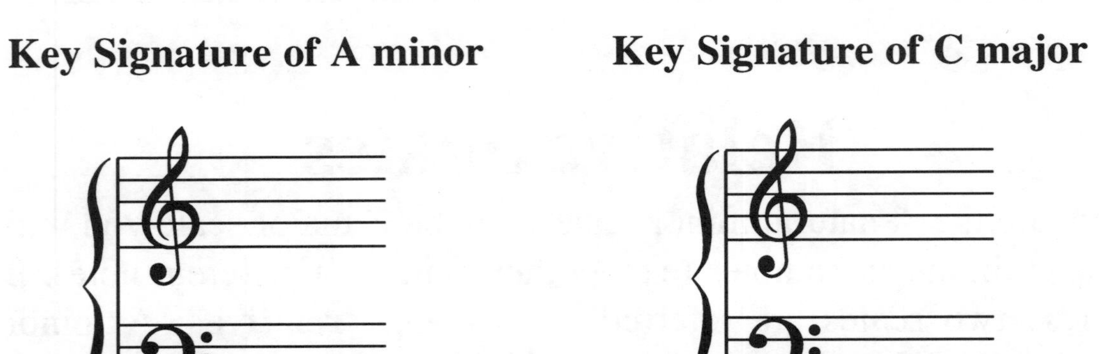

If a song ends with a minor chord it is most likely to be in a minor key. E.g. Harem Dance on page 22 ends in an Am chord and is in the key of Am. Minka on page 29 ends in an Em chord and is in the key of Em.

22. E Natural Minor Scale

You will notice that the notes in the E natural minor scale are the same as the notes in the G major scale. E minor is the relative minor of G major and shares the same key signature (one sharp, F♯).

Key Signature of E minor **Key Signature of G major**

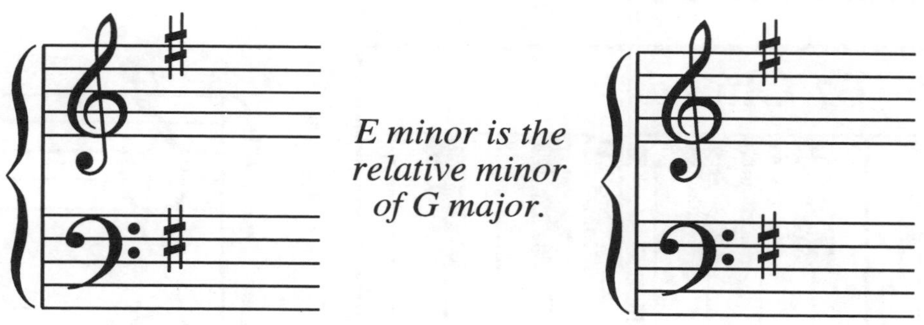

The E minor Chord (Em)

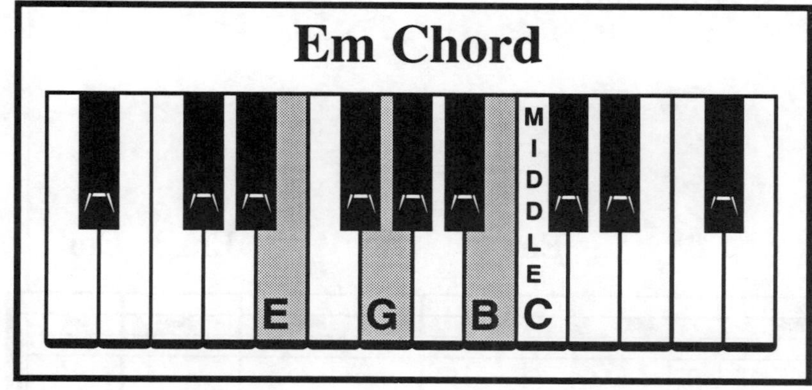

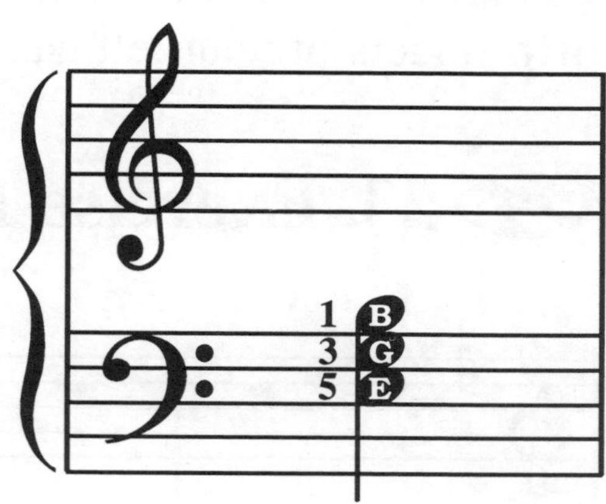

To play the Em chord use the **first**, **third**, and **fifth** finger of your **left** hand as shown in the diagram.

Lesson 8

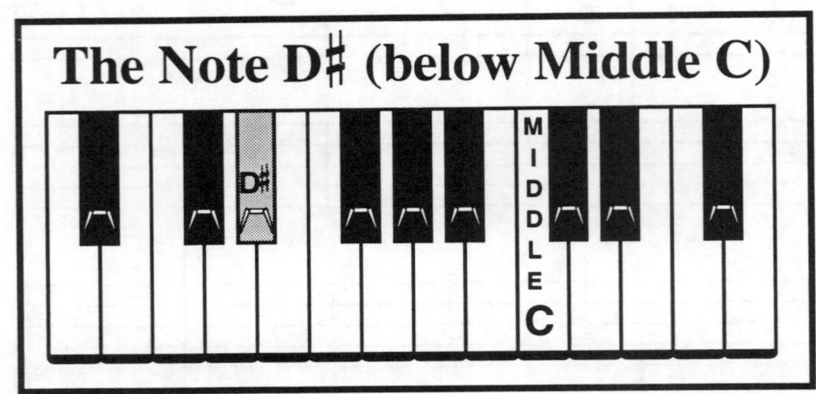

The D♯ note is the black key immediately to the right of the D note as shown in the diagram.

The Note D♯

(below Middle C)

The B7 Chord

The B7 chord contains the D♯ note given above.

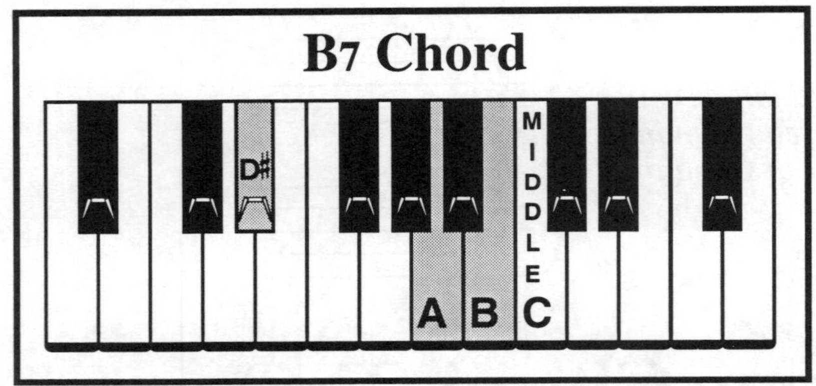

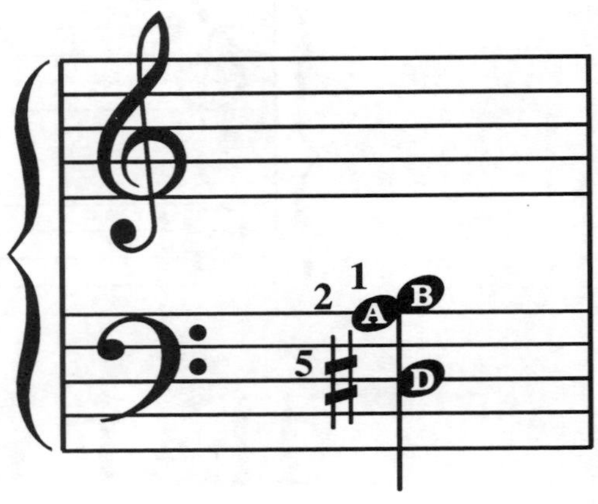

To play the B7 chord use the **first**, **second** and **fifth** fingers of your left hand.

23. Exercise 12

The Harmonic Minor Scale

Another type of minor scale is called the harmonic minor scale. This scale is the same as the natural minor scale except that the seventh note is raised by one semitone (sharpened). E.g., in the A harmonic minor scale the seventh note is G♯, which is the seventh note of the A natural minor scale raised one semitone. This raised seventh note is called the leading note.

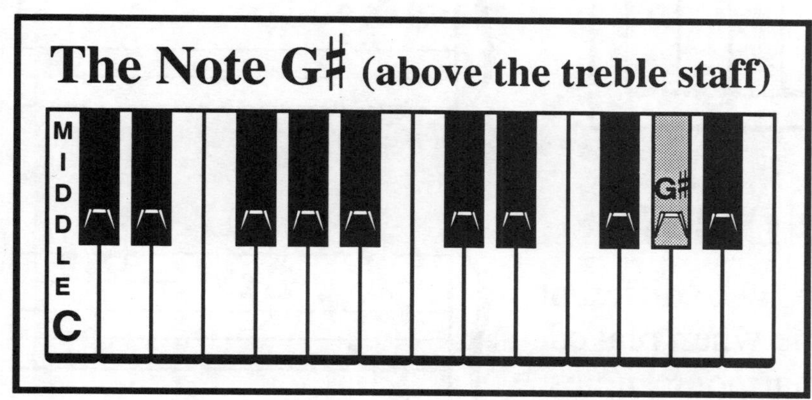

The Note G♯ (above the treble staff)

24. A Harmonic Minor Scale

Lesson 9

The Note D♯
(on the fourth line of the treble staff)

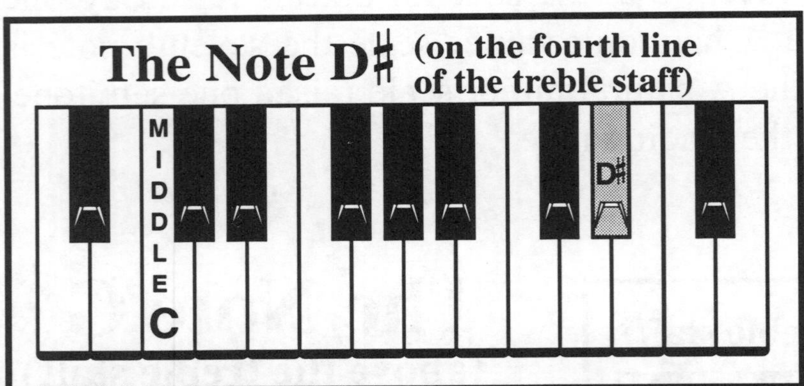

Enharmonic Notes

Certain notes can be written in two different ways, although they sound the same when played. Such notes are referred to as enharmonic notes. E.g. the note D♯ has the same position on the keyboard as the note E♭, so D♯ and E♭ are said to be enharmonic notes. There are further examples of enharmonic notes in the following lessons.

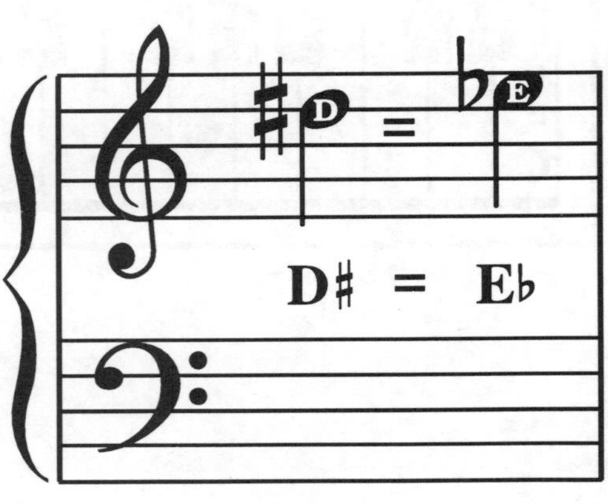

 Exercise 25

26. E Harmonic Minor Scale

The leading note of the E harmonic minor scale is D♯. The leading note of a harmonic minor scale is never indicated in the key signature.

27. Minka

Traditional

The key signature for Em contains one sharp (F♯). This is the same key signature as G major. Em is the relative minor key of G major. Because the above song ends in an Em chord, it is in the key of E minor. Another way of determining if a song is in a major key or its relative minor is to look for the leading note in the melody (ie the sharpened 7th note contained in the harmonic minor scale). The song Minka contains the leading note of the E harmonic minor scale (D♯) which is another indication that this song is in the key of Em.

Lesson 10

The D minor chord (Dm)

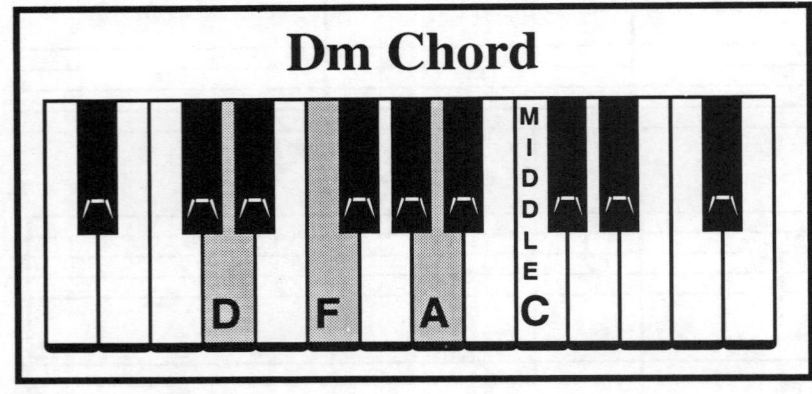

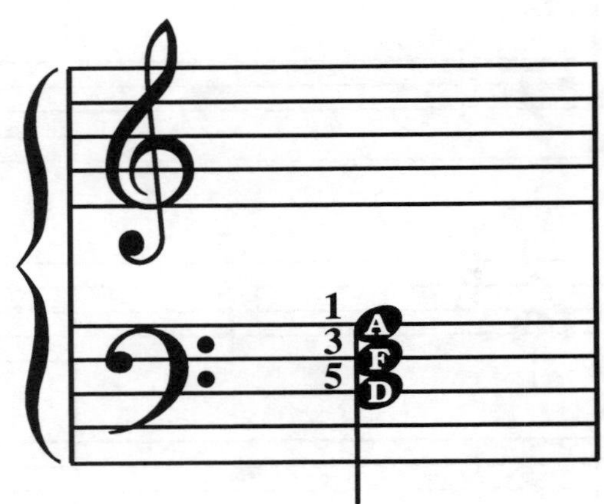

To play the D minor chord use the **first**, **third** and **fifth** fingers of your **left** hand.

Exercise 28

Exercise 29

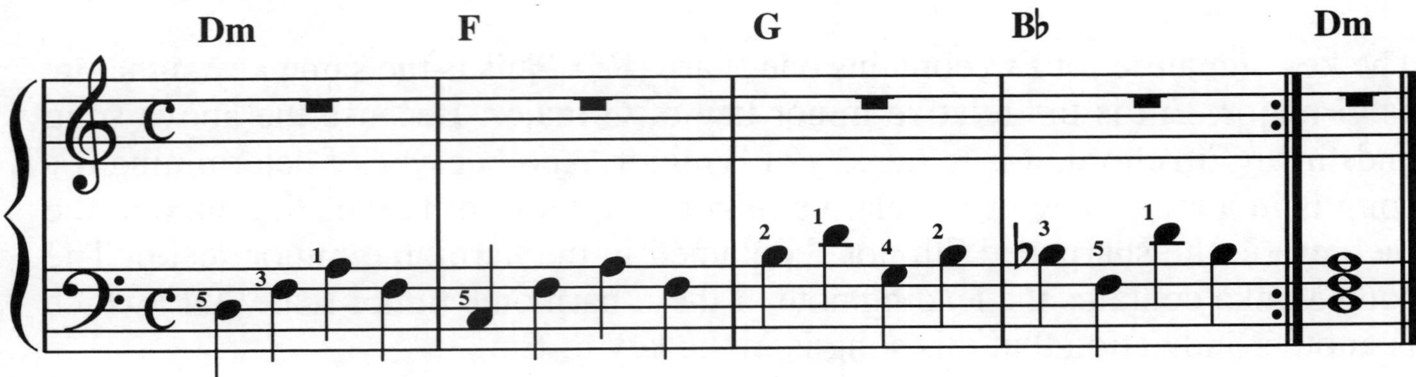

30. D Natural Minor Scale

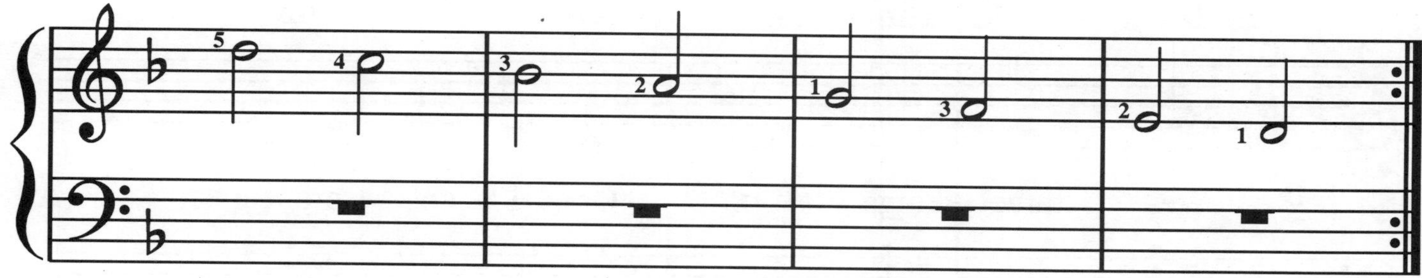

31. D Harmonic Minor Scale

The leading note of the D harmonic minor scale is C♯.

The key signature for Dm contains one flat (B♭). This is the same key signature as F major. D minor is the relative minor of F major.

Key Signature of D minor

Modulation

Modulation is when there is a key change within a piece of music. E.g. the song We Three Kings of Orient Are starts in the key of Dm but modulates to the key of F major in bar 17, and stays in that key until the end of the song.

32. We Three Kings of Orient Are

Traditional

Dm Dm A7 Dm

We three kings of Or - i - ent are

1 2 3 4

Dm Dm A7 Dm

Bear - ing gifts we tra - vel a - far.

5 6 7 8

Dm C7 F F

Field and foun - tain, moor and moun - tain,

9 10 11 12

C7 A7 Dm C7

foll - ow - ing yon - der star. O________

13 14 15 16

F
F
B♭
F
Star of won - der, star of might,
17
18
19
20
F
F
B♭
F
Star with roy - al beau - ty bright,
21
22
23
24
F
C7
B♭
C7
West - ward lead - ing, still pro - ceed - ing,
25
26
27
28
F
F
B♭
F
guide us to thy per - fect light.
29
30
31
32

Lesson 11

The A minor chord
(second inversion)

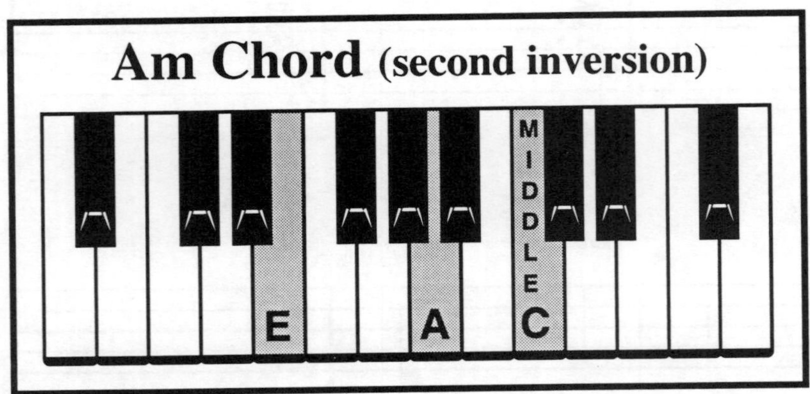

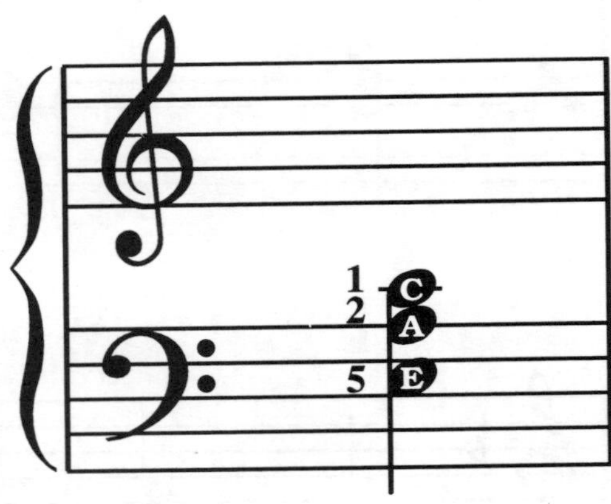

To play this Am chord use the **first**, **second** and **fifth** fingers of your **left** hand.

This Am chord is the second inversion of the root position Am chord given on page 21.

 Exercise 33

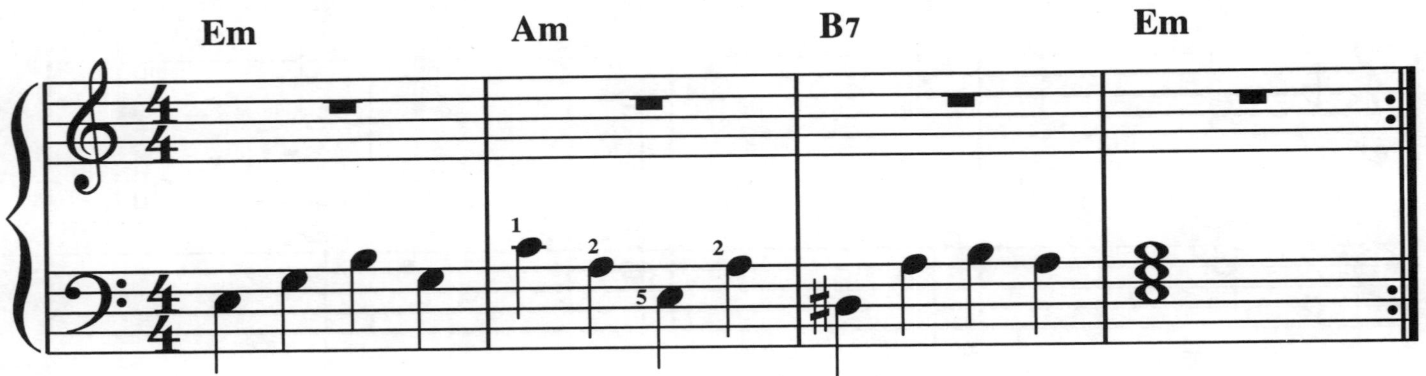

34. When Johnny Comes Marching Home

On the recording there are **five** beats to introduce this song.

Traditional

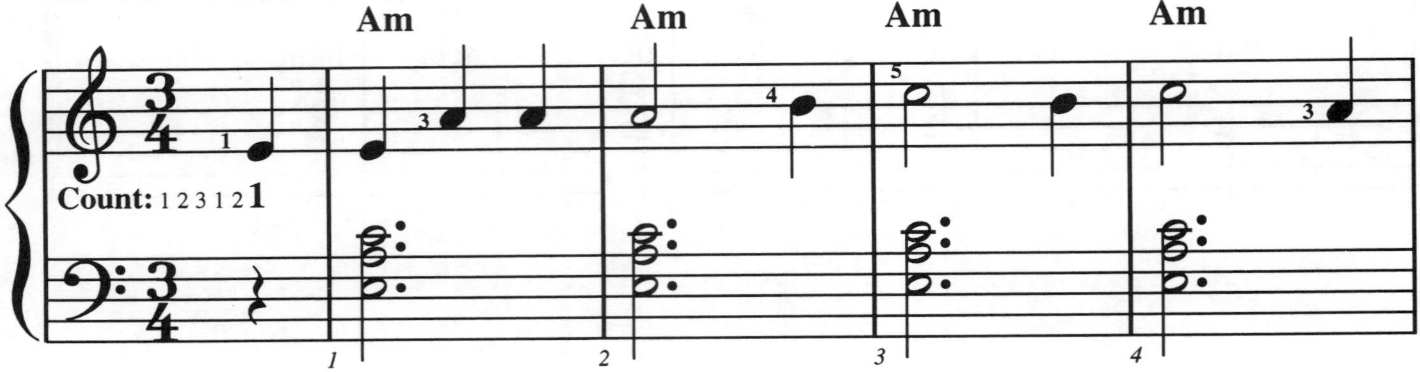

Em
Em
Em
Em
Am
Am
Am
Am
C
C
E7
E7
Am
Am
E7
E7
Am
Am
E7
E7
Am
E7
Am
E7
Am
Am
Am

Lesson 12

The D minor chord (Dm)

(second inversion)

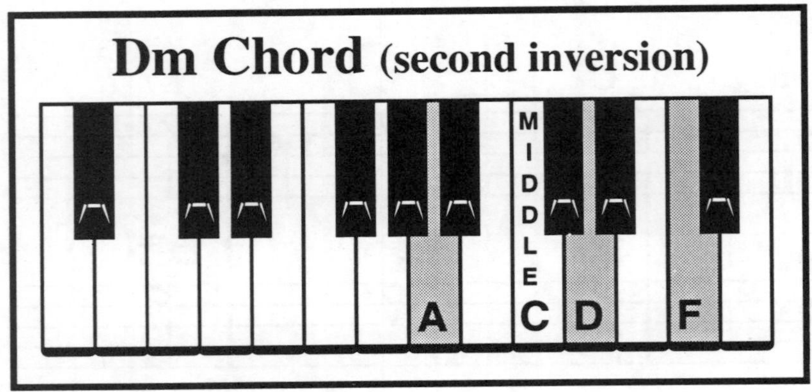

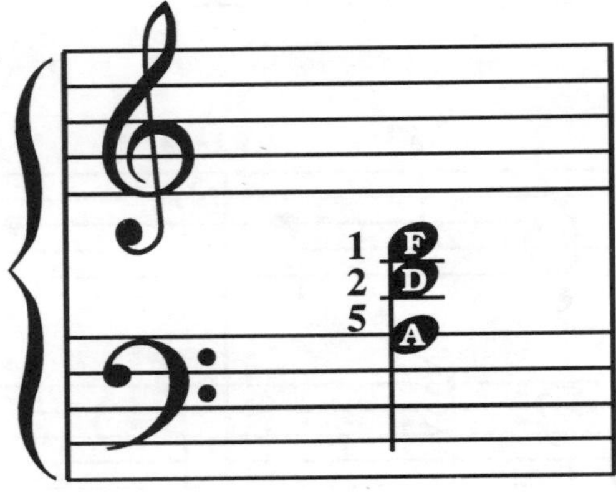

To play this Dm chord use the **first**, **second** and **fifth** fingers of your **left** hand.

This Dm chord is the second inversion of the root position Dm chord shape given on page 30.

35. Volga Boatman

Traditional

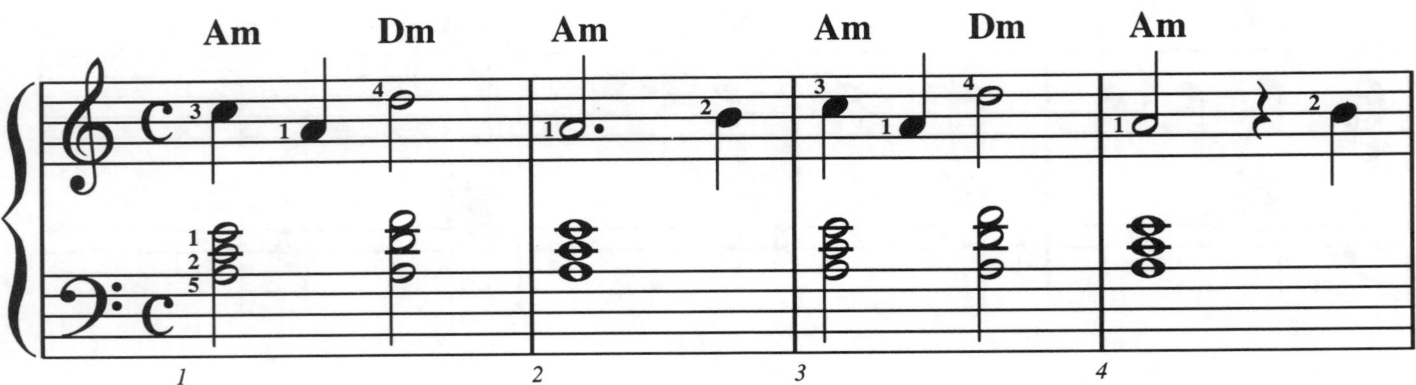

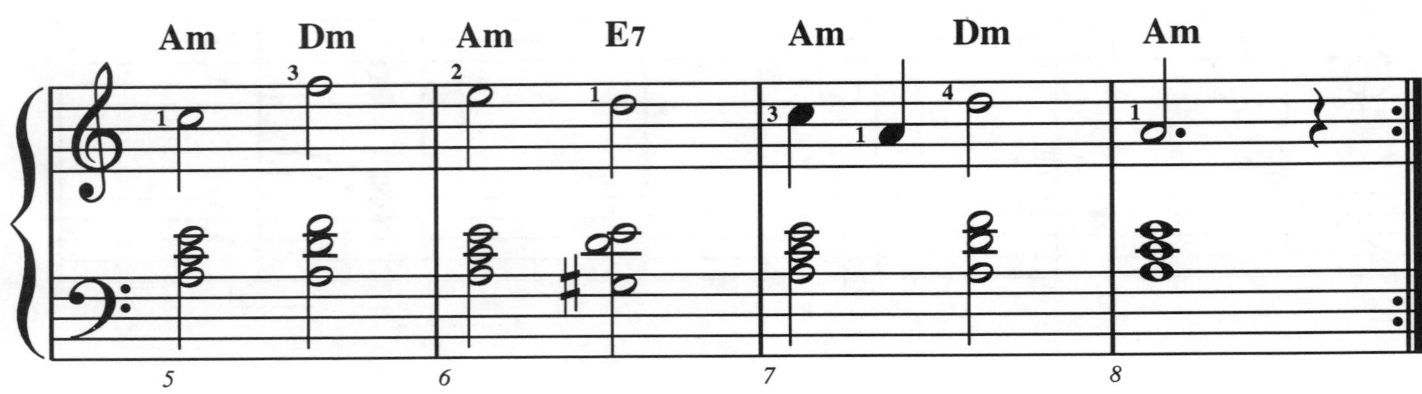

The E minor chord (Em)
(first inversion)

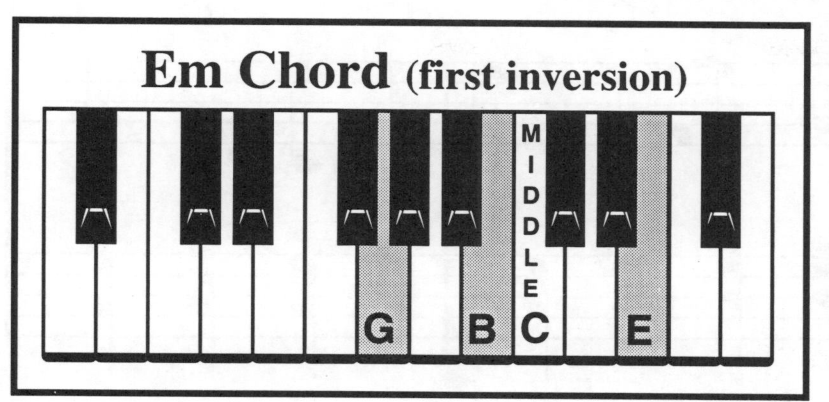

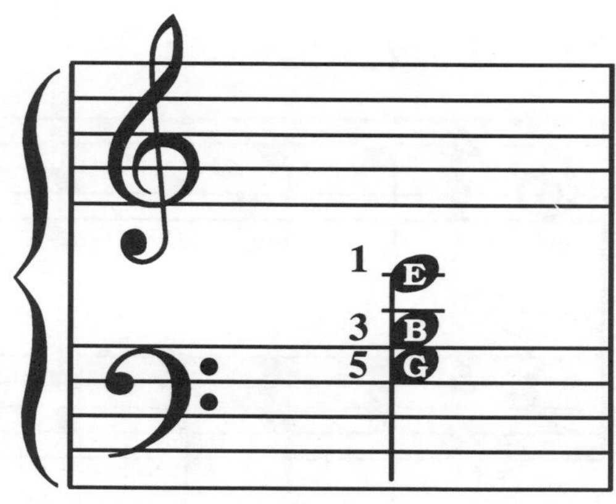

To play this Em chord use the **first**, **third** and **fifth** fingers of your **left** hand.

This Em chord is the first inversion of the root position Em chord shape given on page 25.

Turnaround Progressions

In Lesson 5, you were introduced to the 12 bar blues chord progression. Another very important chord progression to learn is called the **turnaround**. Like 12 bar blues, it is the basis of many songs, and it will probably sound familiar to you also.

36. Turnaround in the Key of C

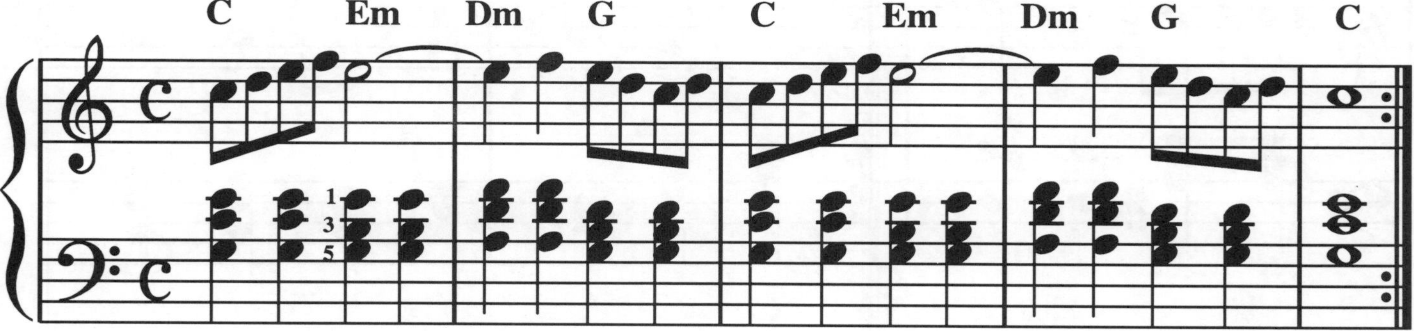

37. Turnaround in the Key of G

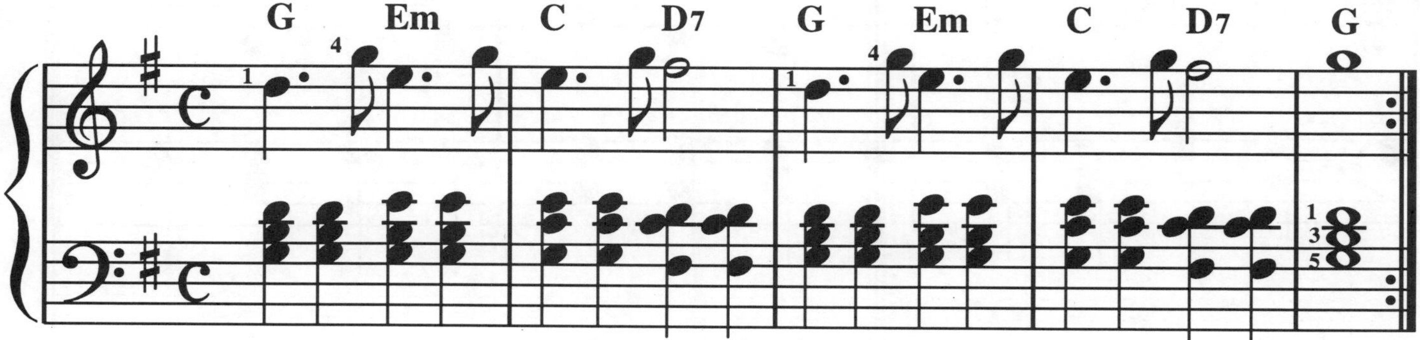

38. English Country Gardens

Traditional

Lesson 13

Syncopation

Syncopation is the accenting of a beat which is normally unaccented. In $\frac{4}{4}$ time, accents normally occur on the downbeats (the whole numbered beats) in each bar. The first and third beats are more emphasised than the second and fourth beats. Syncopation occurs when accents are played on one or more of the upbeats (the beats in between the whole numbered beats) in the bar, ie, on the "and" count.

Exercise 39

In this exercise, syncopation occurs in each bar. Emphasis is given to the "and" count between the first and second beats by the note which commences on that count.

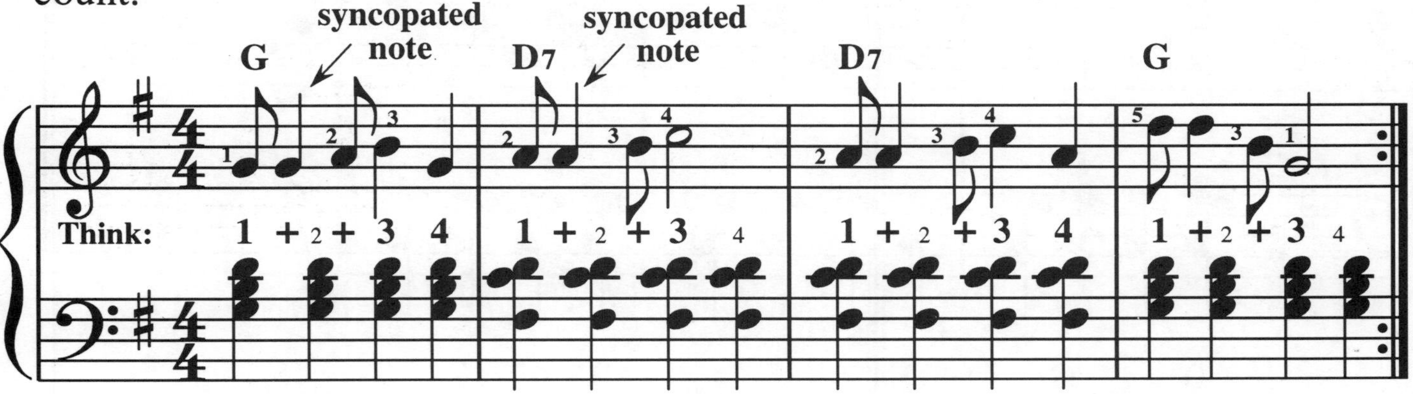

40. Strike Up the Band

Traditional

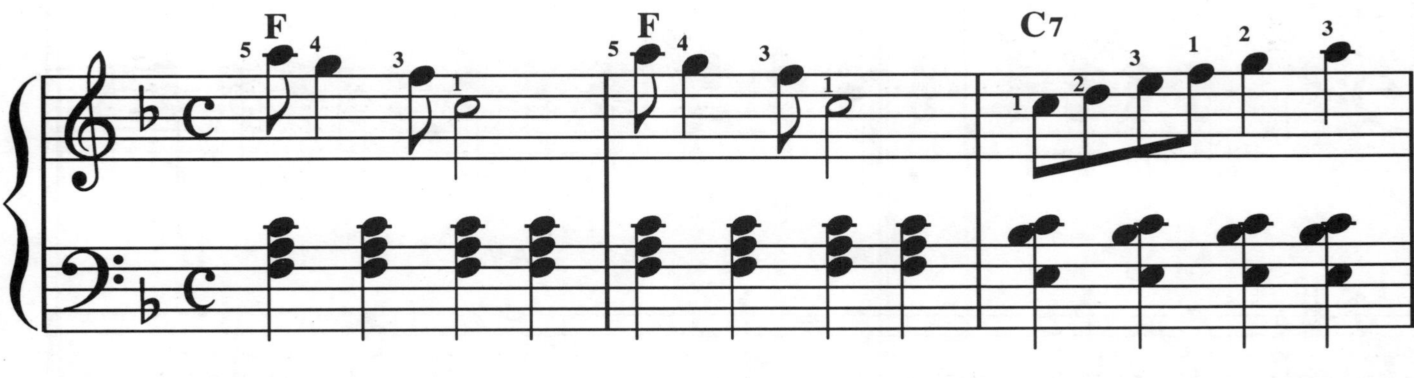

41. Under the Bamboo Tree

Traditional

On the recording there are **three** beats to introduce this song.

Lesson 14

The Sixteenth Note

This is a **sixteenth note**. Its value is one quarter of a beat. There are sixteen sixteenth notes in one bar of $\frac{4}{4}$ time. Sixteenth notes usually occur in groups of two or four.

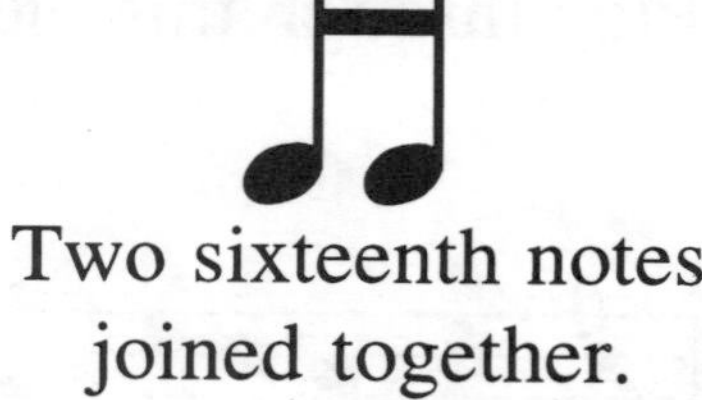

Two sixteenth notes joined together.

Four sixteenth notes joined together.

Exercise 42

Exercise 43

44. Arkansas Traveller

Traditional

Play through this piece **very slowly** at first and be careful with your timing.

Lesson 15

The Dotted Eighth Note

A dot written after a note lengthens the note by half its value.

An eighth note with a dot written after it has a value of three quarters of a beat, or three sixteenth notes tied together.

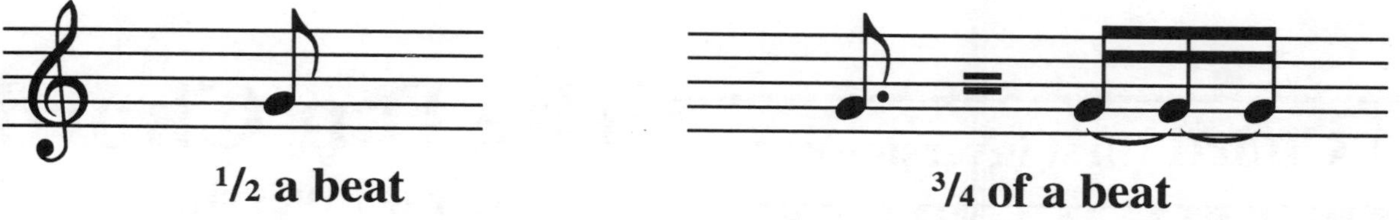

A dotted eighth note is usually followed by a sixteenth note.

The dotted eighth note will sound most effective when you play it as if the dot were underneath the note instead of after it. Play it short and leave a gap between the dotted note and the following sixteenth note.

45. Funeral March

Frederic Chopin

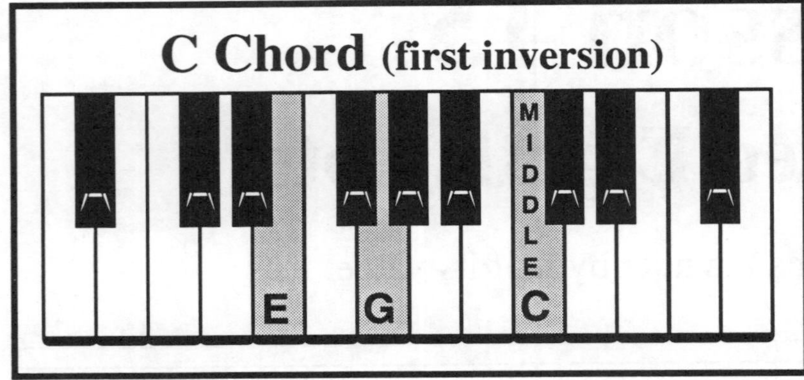

To play this first inversion C chord use the **first**, **third** and **fifth** fingers of the **left** hand.

The C Chord
(first inversion)

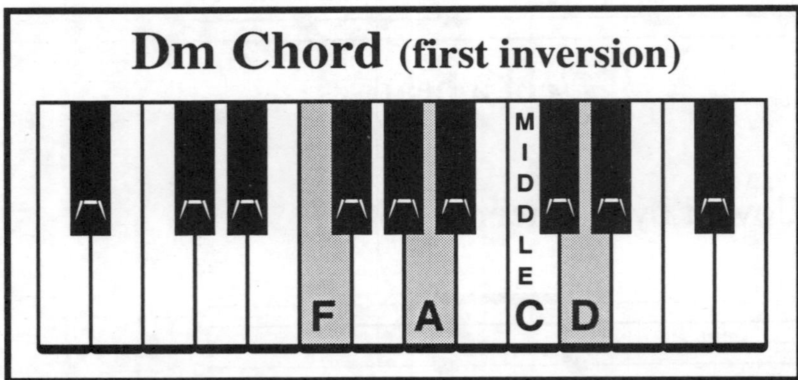

To play this first inversion Dm chord use the **first**, **third** and **fifth** fingers of the **left** hand.

The Dm Chord
(first inversion)

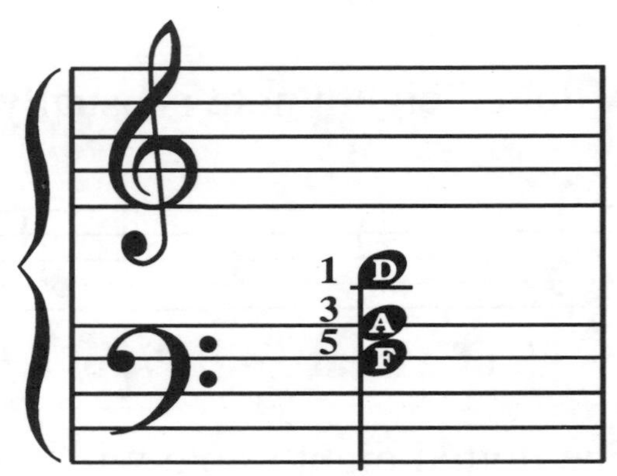

Exercise 46

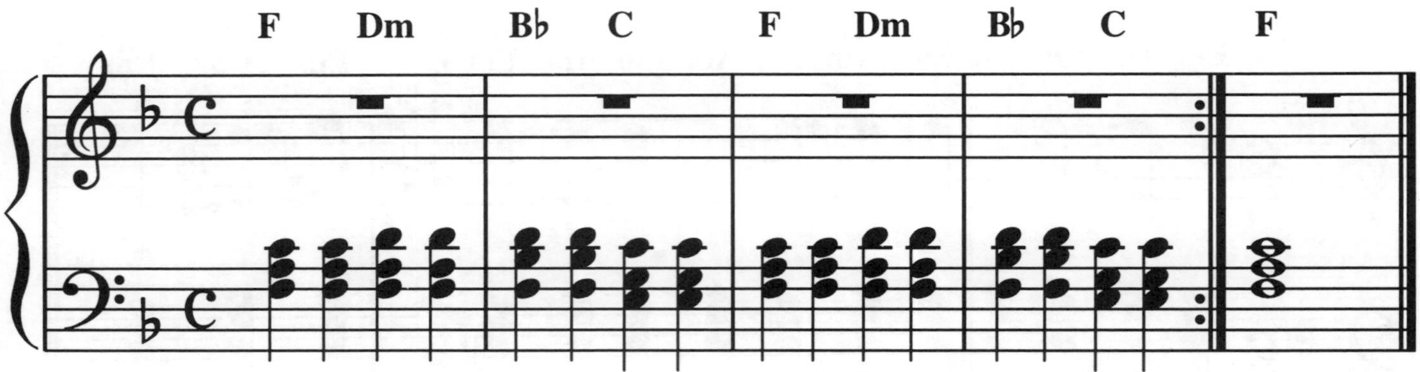

The Eighth Rest

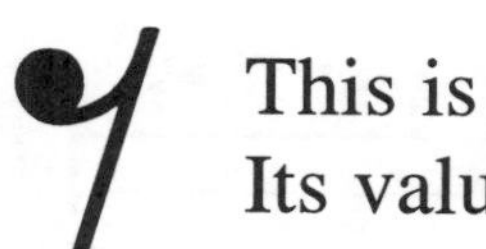

This is an **eighth** rest.
Its value is **half a beat**.

Count: 1 + 2 + 3 + 4 +

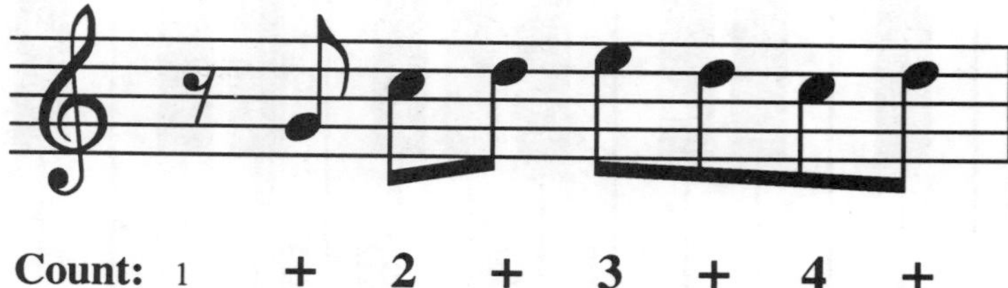

In the song 1812 Overture, there is an eighth rest at the beginning of bars 1, 3, 5 and 7. Do not start playing the melody until the "and" count between the first and second beats.

47. The 1812 Overture

Peter Tschaikowsky

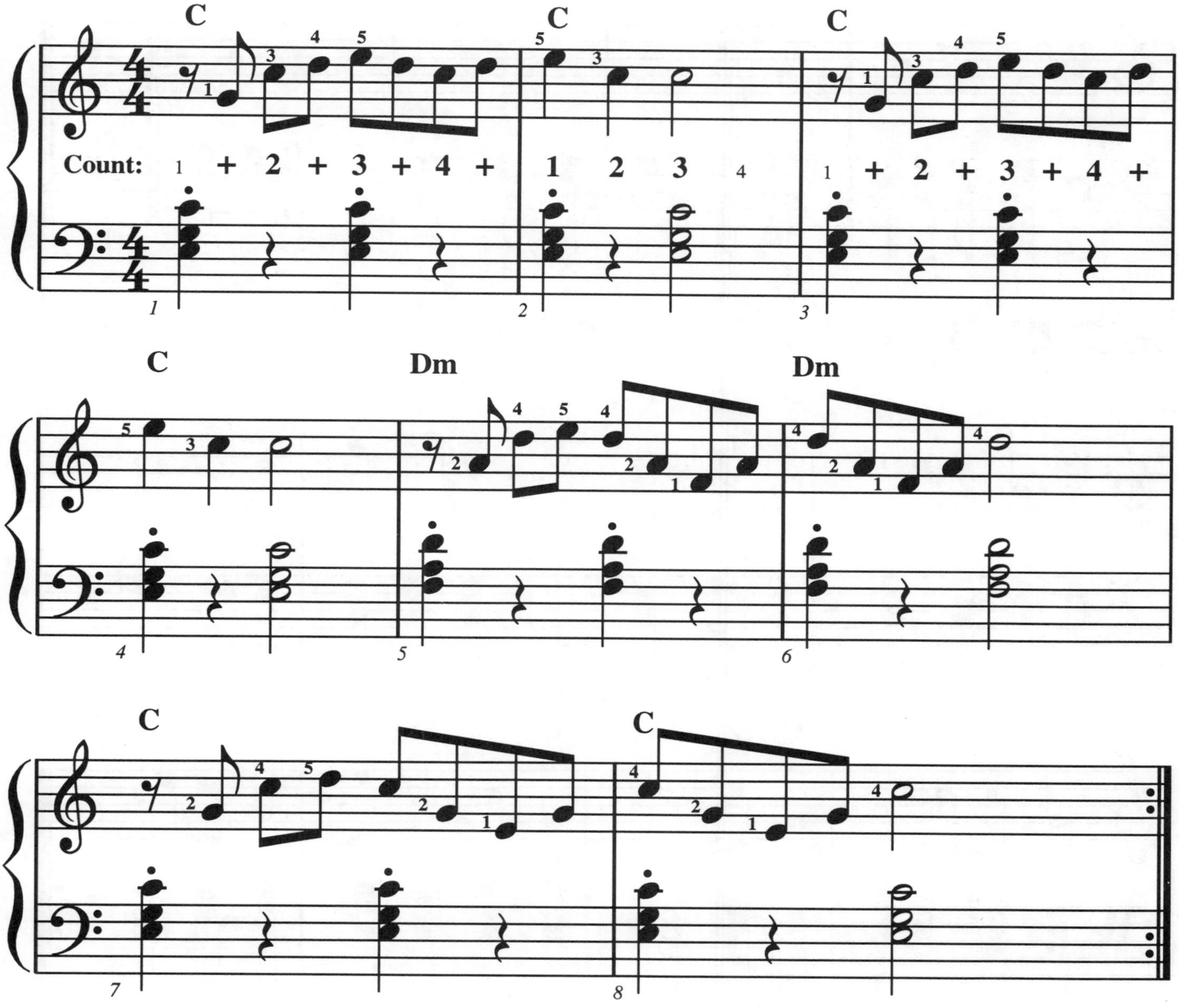

C
C
C
Count: 1 + 2 + 3 + 4 +
1 2 3 4
1 + 2 + 3 + 4 +
C
Dm
Dm
C
C

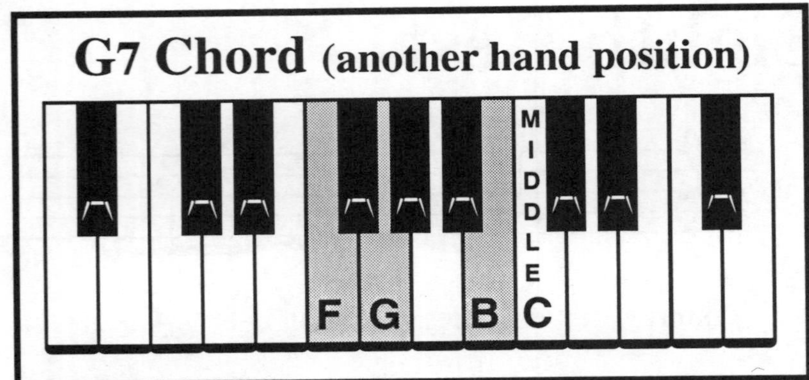

The G7 Chord
(another hand position)

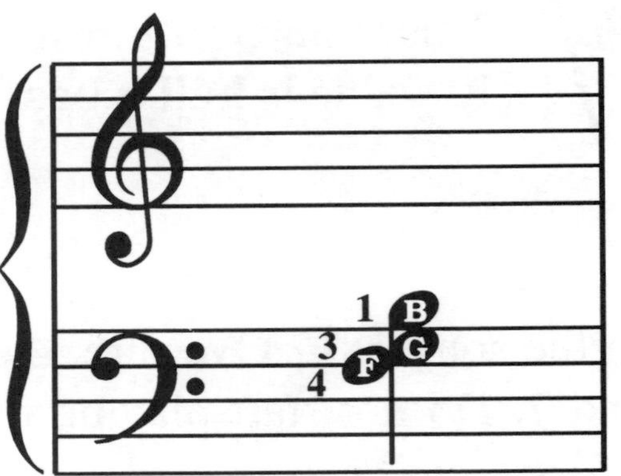

To play this G seventh chord use the **thumb**, **third** and **fourth** fingers of your **left** hand.

Exercise 48

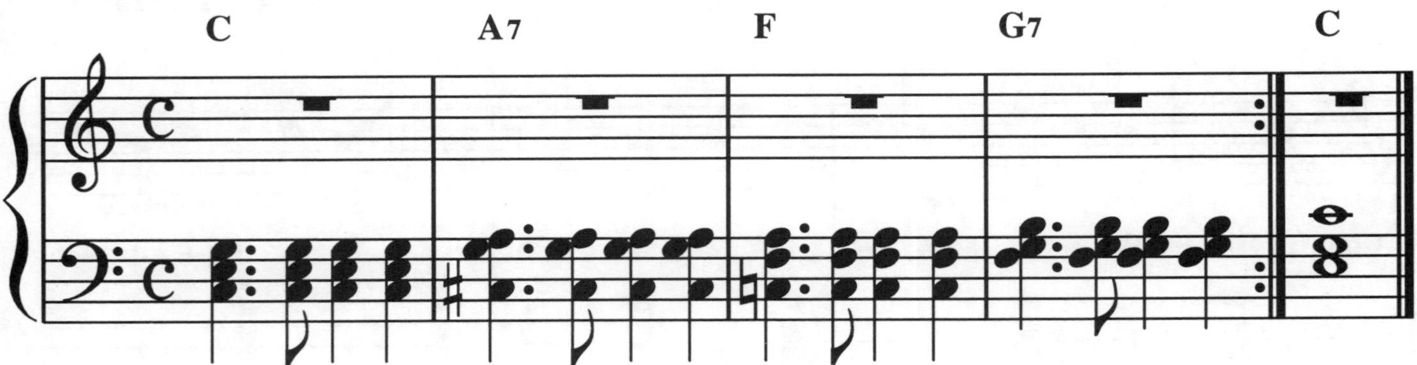

49. Here Comes the Bride

R. Wagner

Lesson 16

The $\frac{6}{8}$ (Six Eight) Time Signature

So far you have used three time signatures $\frac{3}{4}$, $\frac{4}{4}$ and C.

In this lesson you will learn a new time signature – the $\frac{6}{8}$ time signature.

In any time signature, the number on the top half tell you **how many** beats there are in each bar. E.g., in $\frac{3}{4}$ time, the number 3 tells you that each bar has three beats. In $\frac{6}{8}$ time, the number 6 indicates that there are six beats in each bar.

The number on the bottom half of a time signature tells you **what kind** of beats you are counting. E.g., in $\frac{3}{4}$ time, the number 4 tells you that you are counting quarter note beats. In $\frac{6}{8}$ time, the number 8 indicates that the beats being counted are **eighth note** beats. Thus, each bar of $\frac{6}{8}$ time contains the equivalent of six eighth note beats.

How to Count $\frac{6}{8}$ Time

In $\frac{6}{8}$ time, notes are written in two groups, each with a value of three eighth notes.

A note with a value of two eighth notes can be represented by a quarter note. A note with a value of three eighth notes can be represented by a dotted quarter note.

Slow Tempo $\frac{6}{8}$

If the tempo of the song is slow, it is best to count every beat in the bar, starting with 1 and finishing with 6.

Exercise 50

On the recording there are **six** beats to introduce exercises in slow $\frac{6}{8}$ time.

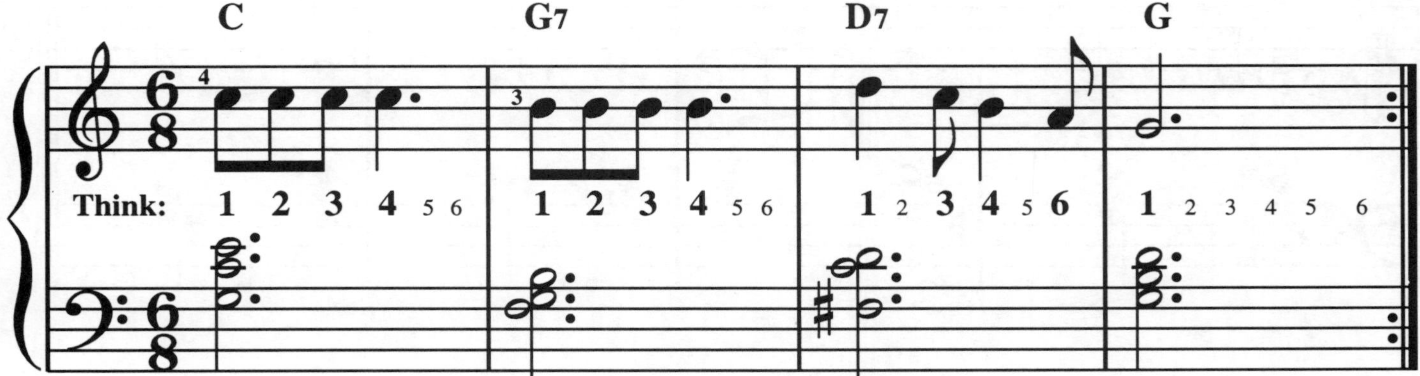

51. The Pleasure of Love

Traditional French

On the recording there are **five** beats to introduce this song.

Fast Tempo $\frac{6}{8}$

In a fast tempo, the six eighth notes in each bar are too fast to count individually, so it is more natural to feel and count only **two** beats per bar – those beats which fall on the first eighth note and the fourth eighth note. You can think of the eighth notes as pulses, and use the term beat to mean a group of three pulses. In fast $\frac{6}{8}$, three eighth note pulses make up one beat.

This is why the notes in $\frac{6}{8}$ time are grouped in batches of three eighth notes. It is so that your eye can easily see where the beats fall when the tempo is quick.

When you are counting two beats per bar in $\frac{6}{8}$ time, you are counting the eighth notes three at a time. The beat value is then three eighth notes, for one dotted quarter note.

Exercise 52 *Fast*

On the recording there are **four** beats to introduce exercises in fast $\frac{6}{8}$ time.

53. The Irish Washerwoman

Traditional

C C G7 G7

Count: 1 2 + a

C C G7 C

54. Mexican Hat Dance

Traditional Mexican

* The term **D.C. al Fine**, which stands for Da Capo al Fine, means that you play the song again from the start until you reach the word Fine (bar 9).

Lesson 17

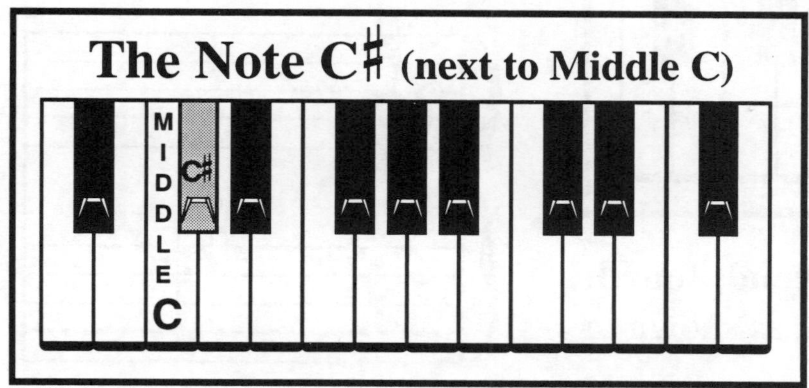

The Note C♯
(next to Middle C)

The note C♯ is the black key immediately to the right of Middle C.

55. Mexican Dance

Traditional Mexican

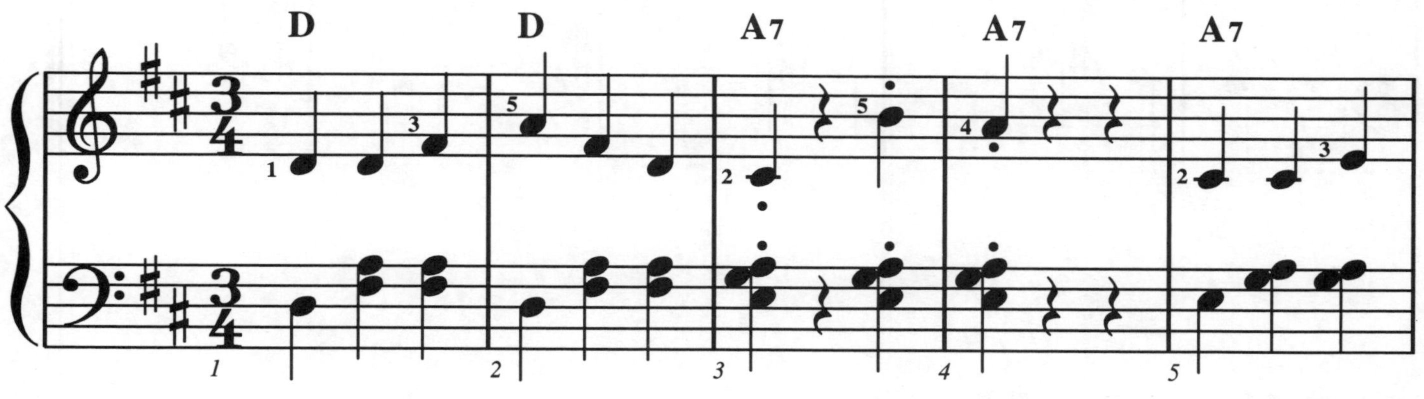

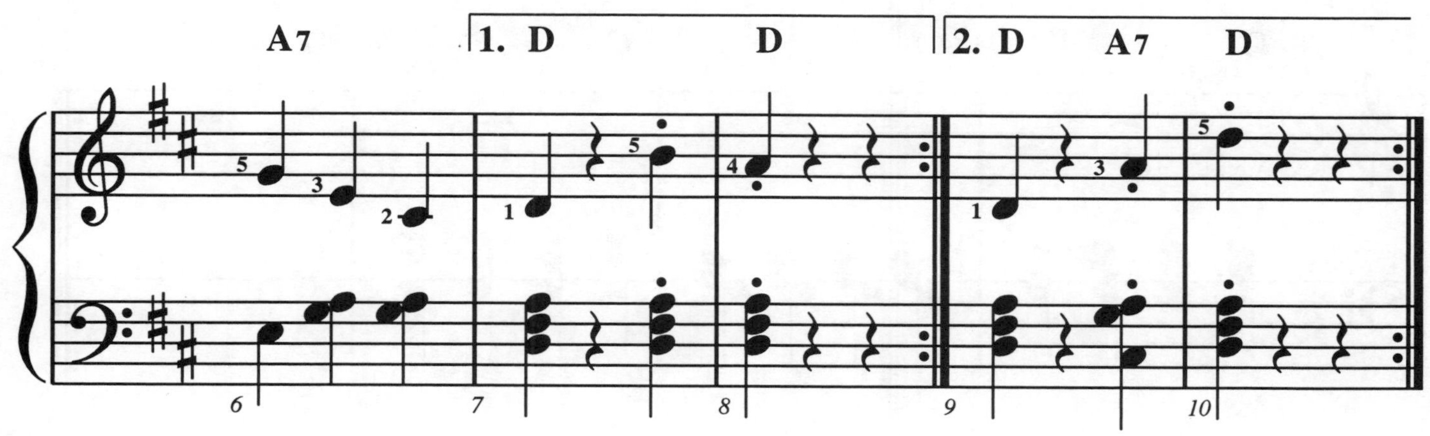

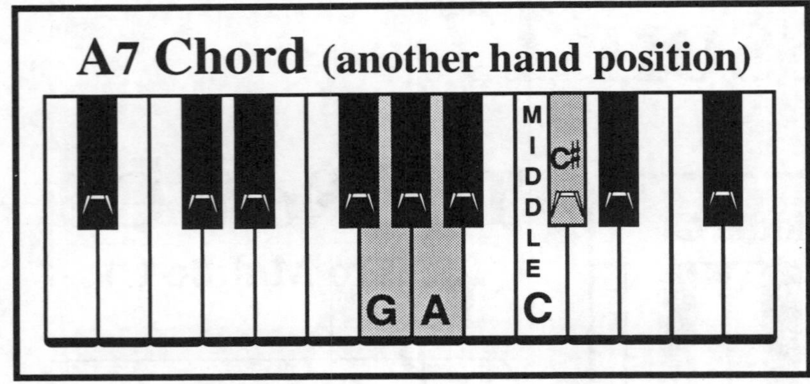

The A7 Chord
(another hand position)

To play the A7 chord, use the **second**, **fourth** and **fifth** fingers of your **left** hand, as shown in the diagram.

Exercise 56

Exercise 57

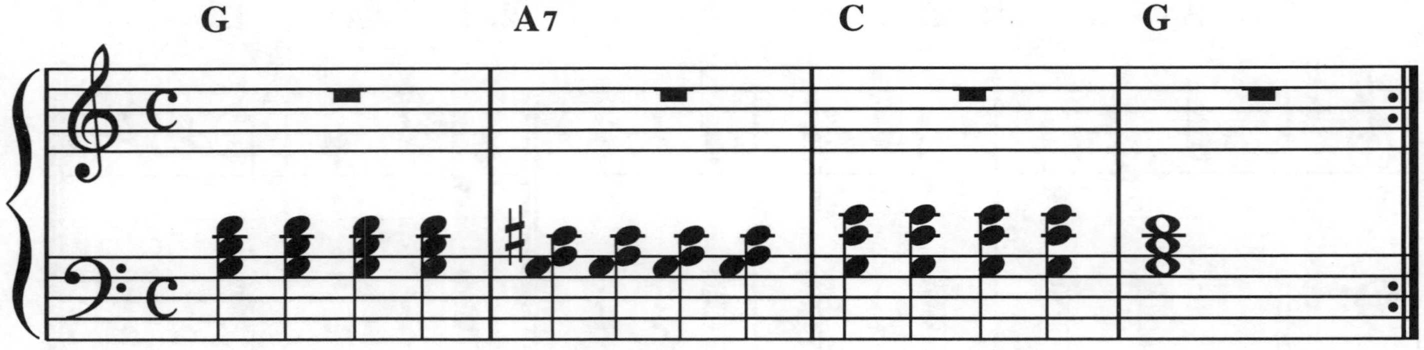

58. Lavender's Blue

Traditional

Lesson 18

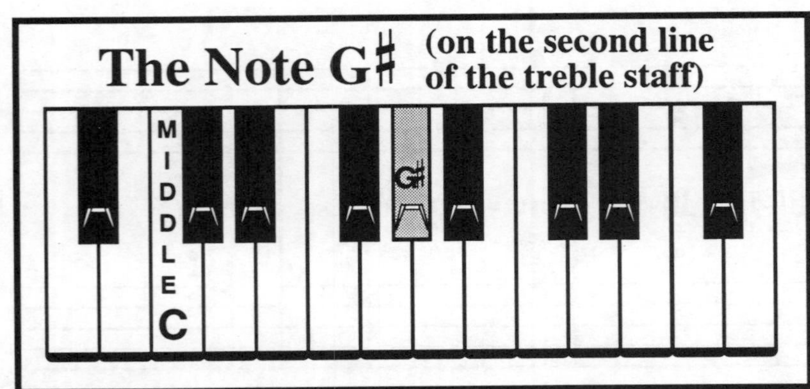

The Note G♯
(on the second line of the treble staff)

The note G♯ is the black key immediately to the right of the G note as shown in the diagram.

59. El Condor Pasa

Traditional South American

This song is written using notes from the A harmonic minor scale, and is in the key of A minor. On the recording there are **four** beats to introduce this song.

Am C C

Count: 1 2 3 4 +

1 2 3

C Am Am

4 5 6

Am C C

7 8 9

C Am Am
10 11 12
F F C C
13 14 15 16
F F C C
17 18 19 20
Am Am Am C
21 22 23 24
C C Am Am
25 26 27 28

Lesson 19

The Note D♯ (E♭)
(below the treble staff)

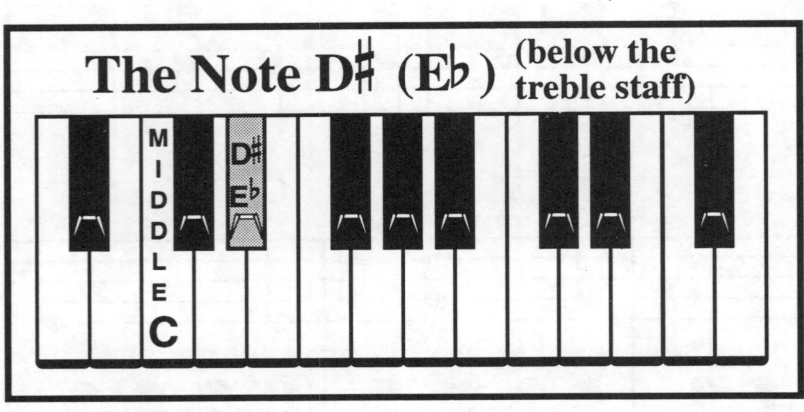

The note D♯ is the black key immediately to the right of the D note as shown in the diagram.

D♯ and E♭ are enharmonic notes.

60. Creepy Blues

This song is a 12 bar blues. It contains sharp, flat and natural signs.

The symbol 𝄐 in bar 14 is called a **pause** or **fermata**. It means that you can sustain the note for as long as you wish.

F
F
C
C
G7
F
1. C
C
2. C
C
C7

Lesson 20

The ₵ (Cut Time) Signature

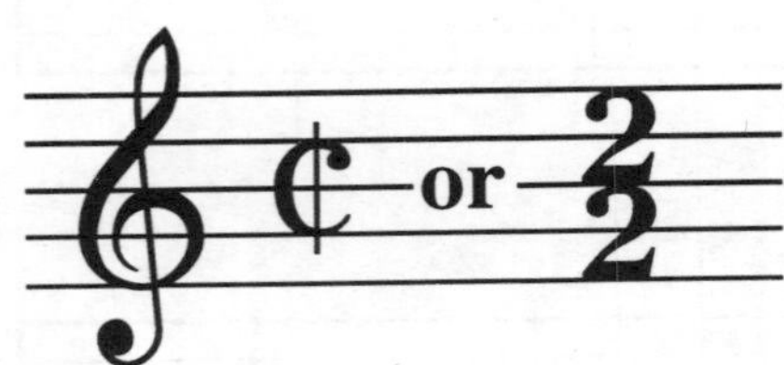

In this lesson you will learn another new time signature – the **cut time signature**. Cut time is sometimes written as 2/2 (two two), but it appears more frequently as ₵ .

In Lesson 16 you saw that the number on the top half of a time signature tells you **how many** beats there are in each bar. Therefore, in 2/2 time the number 2 tells you that each bar has two beats.

The number on the bottom half of a time signature tells you **what kind** of beats you are counting. Thus, in 2/2 or ₵ time, the number 2 tells you that you are counting half note beats.

How to Count ₵ Time

The table below compares note and rest values in C time with values in ₵ or 2/2 time.

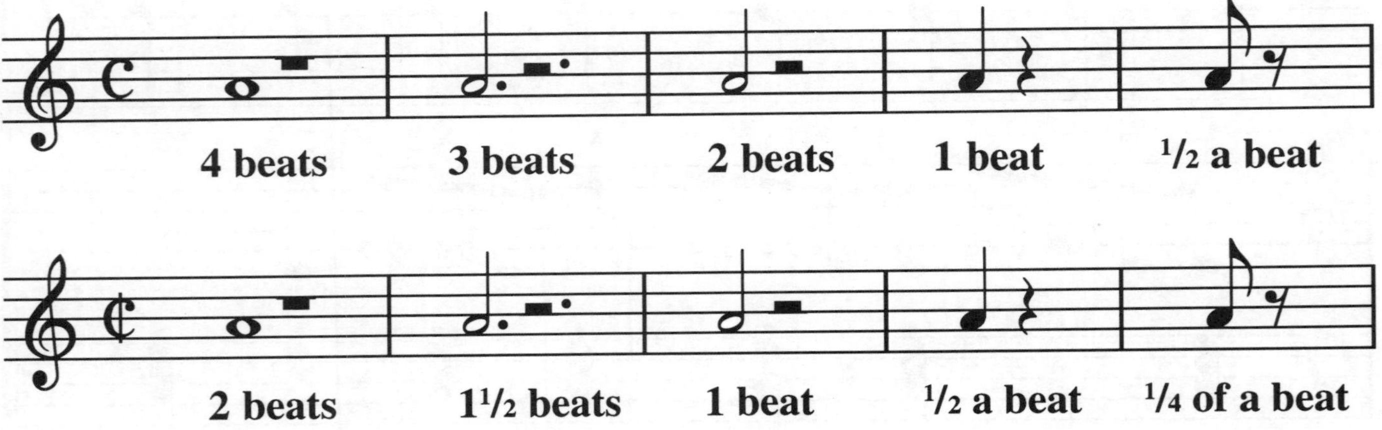

Exercise 61

F Dm B♭ C F Dm B♭ C F

Count: 1 2 1 2 1 2 1 2 1 2

62. Hello My Baby

Traditional

Lesson 21

The Triplet

A triplet is a group of three notes played in the same time as two notes of the same kind. E.g., an **eighth note triplet** consists of three eighth notes played in the same time as you would play two eighth notes. Eighth note triplets are indicated by three eighth notes grouped together by a curved line and the numeral 3, as shown above. Triplets are easy to understand once you have heard them played. Listen to the recording.

Exercise 63

64. Triplet March

65. Amazing Grace

Traditional

On the recording there are five **beats** to introduce this song.

Lesson 22
Swing Rhythms

A **swing rhythm** can be created by tying together the first and second notes of an eighth note triplet. Play Exercise 66 which contains triplets.

Exercise 66

Exercise 67

Exercise 67 has the first and second notes of the triplet group tied. Do not play the second note of the triplet group. Play the first and third notes only. This gives the exercise a 'swing feel'.

Exercise 68

The two eighth note triplets tied together in Exercise 67 can be replaced by a quarter note.

Exercise 69 ♫ = ♩ ♪ (3)

To simplify notation, it is usual to replace the ♩ ♪ (3) with ♫, and to write at the start of the piece, ♫ = ♩ ♪ (3) as illustrated in Exercise 69.

Exercises 67, 68 and 69 sound exactly the same, but are just written differently.

70. By the Light of the Silvery Moon

Traditional

On the recording there are **three** beats to introduce this song.

Lesson 23

More Enharmonic Notes

In Lesson 9 you were introduced to enharmonic notes, i.e. notes that are written in two different ways but sound the same when played.

Written below are some more enharmonic notes that you should become familiar with.

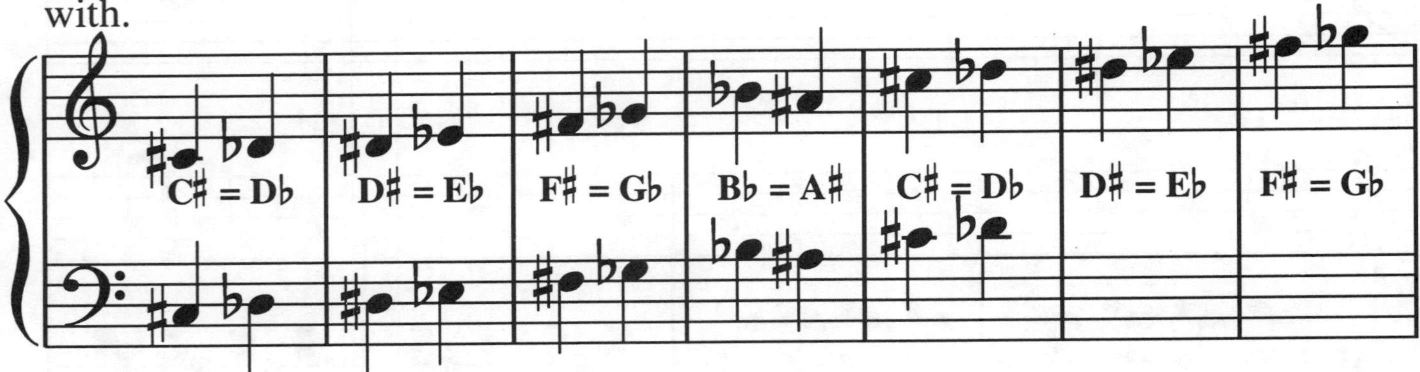

The Chromatic Scale

The interval between a black key and a white key on the piano is known as a semitone and is the smallest interval on the keyboard. A chromatic scale is a sequence of semitones. Each note is one semitone higher or lower than the note before or after it.

71. C Chromatic Scale

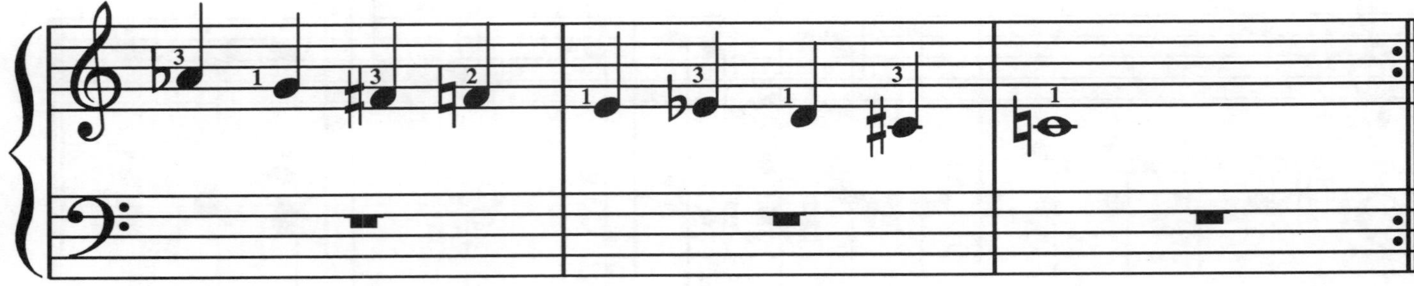

72. Minuet in G

Ludwig van Beethoven

On the recording there are **five** beats to introduce this song.

Lesson 24

The F♯ Diminished Chord

So far you have learnt how to play major, minor and seventh chords. Another type of chord you will need to know is the diminished chord. The diminished chord is indicated by either 'dim' or 'o' e.g C dim or C°. A full summary of diminished chord shapes can be found in the chord chart at the end of this book.

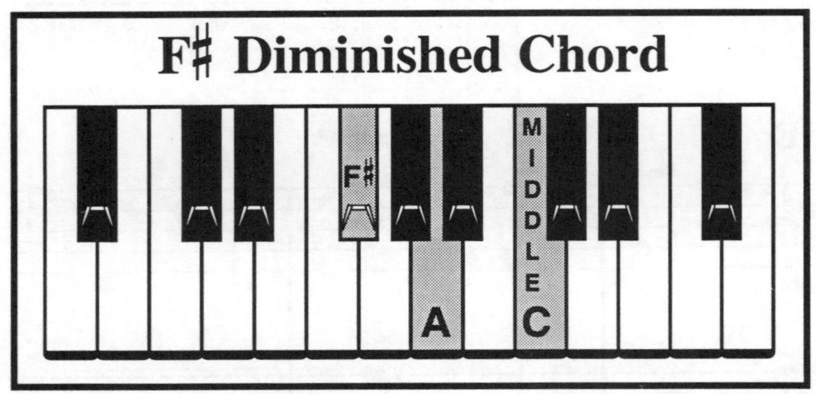

To play the F♯ diminished chord use the **thumb**, **third** and **fourth** finger of your **left** hand.

Exercise 73

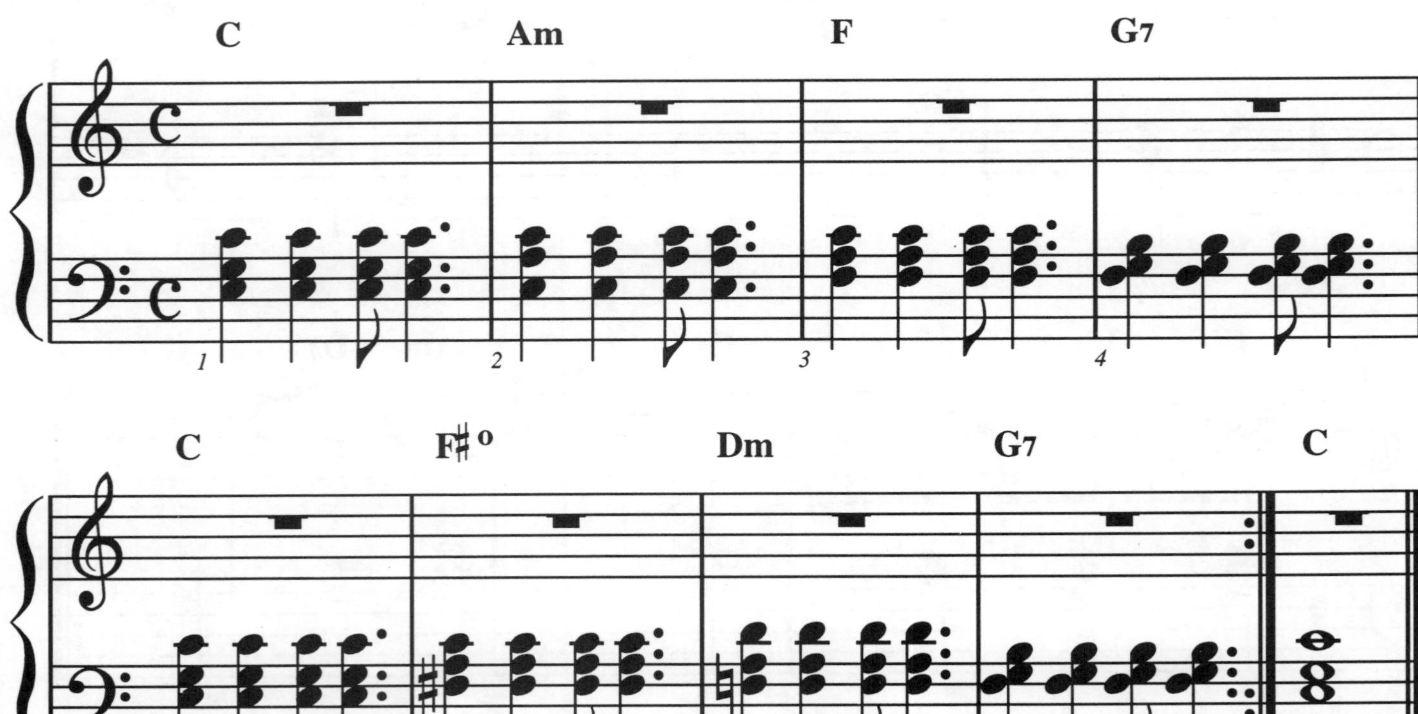

74. Ballin' the Jack

Traditional

75. The Entertainer

Scott Joplin

On the recording there are **three** beats to introduce this song.

*Fm chord - see chord chart on page 73.

Lesson 25

The G Augmented Chord

An augmented chord is indicated by a '+' or 'aug' written after the letter name, e.g. C+ or C aug. A full summary of augmented chord shapes can be found in the chord chart at the end of this book.

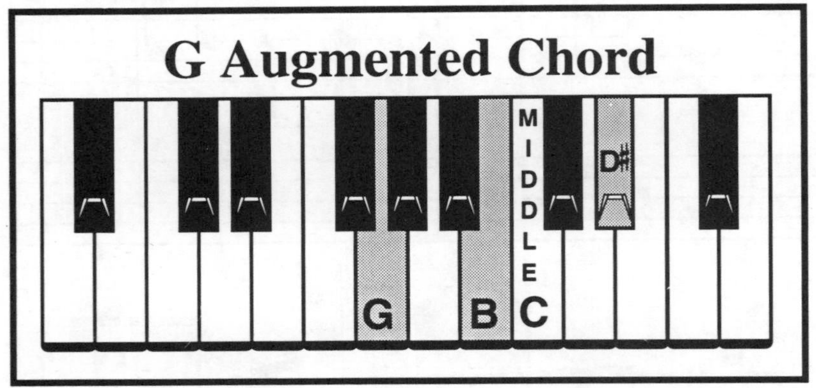

The play the G augmented chord use the **thumb**, **third** and **fifth** fingers of the **left** hand. Move your hand towards the back of the keys to make this chord easier to play.

Exercise 76

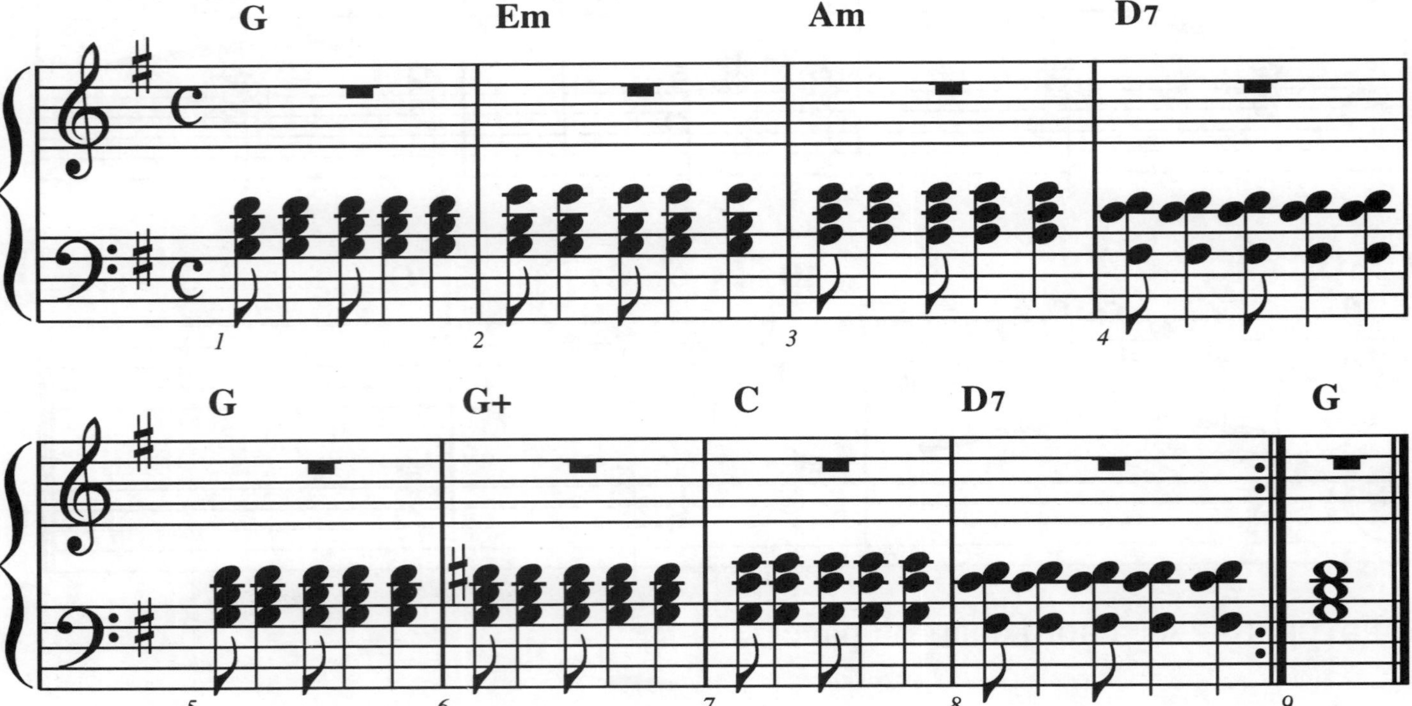

77. Mary's a Grand Old Name
On the recording there are **three** beats to introduce this song.
George M. Cohan
C A7 D7 G G+
For it is Mar - y, Mar - y, Plain as an - y name can
C D7 B7 G D7
be ___ But with pro - pri - e - ty, So - ci - e - ty will
G G+ C C A7
say Ma - rie ___. But it was Mar - y,
D7 G G+ C
Mar - y, Long be-fore the fash - ions came ___, And there is
C A7 Dm D7 G7 C
some-thing there That sounds so square; It's a grand old name.

Major Chord Chart

Chord Name	Notes In Chord	Root Position	1st Inversion	2nd Inversion
C	C E G	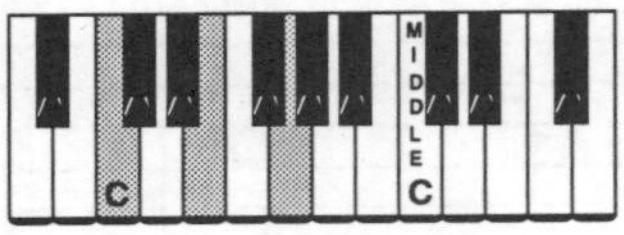		
D♭ (C♯)	D♭ F A♭			
D	D F♯ A	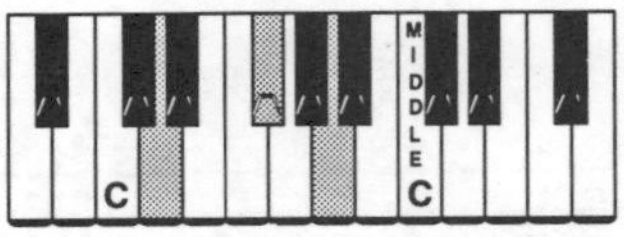		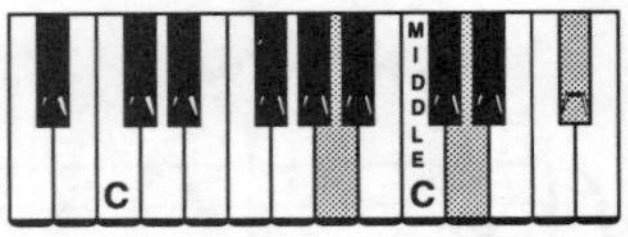
E♭	E♭ G B♭			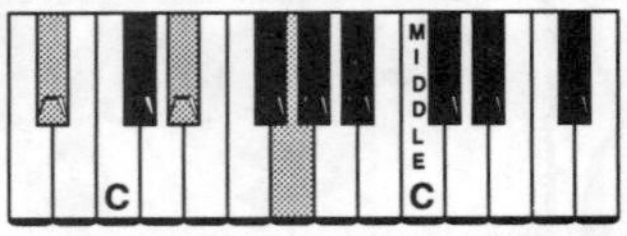
E	E G♯ B			
F	F A C		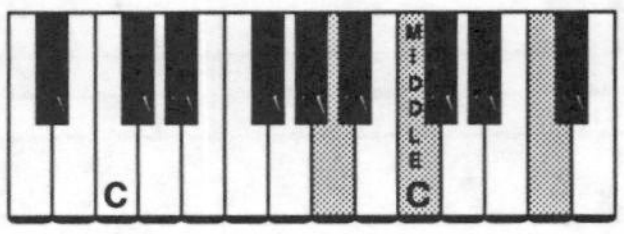	
F♯ (G♭)	F♯ A♯ C♯			
G	G B D			
A♭	A♭ C E♭			
A	A C♯ E			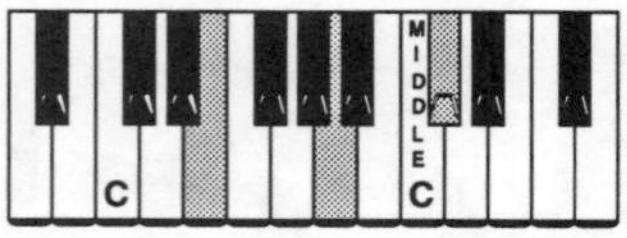
B♭	B♭ D F			
B	B D♯ F♯			

Minor Chord Chart

Chord Name	Notes In Chord	Root Position	1st Inversion	2nd Inversion
Cm	C E♭ G			
C♯m	C♯ E G♯			
Dm	D F A			
E♭m	E♭ G♭ B♭			
Em	E G B			
Fm	F A♭ C			
F♯m	F♯ A C♯			
Gm	G B♭ D			
G♯m	G♯ B D♯			
Am	A C E			
B♭m	B♭ D♭ F			
Bm	B D F♯			

Seventh Chord Chart

Chord Name	Notes In Chord	Root Position	5th Omitted	3rd Omitted
C7	C E G B♭			
D♭7	D♭ F A♭ B			
D7	D F♯ A C			
E♭7	E♭ G B♭ D♭			
E7	E G♯ B D			
F7	F A C E♭			
F♯7 (G♭7)	F♯ A♯ C♯ E			
G7	G B D F			
A♭7	A♭ C E♭ F♯			
A7	A C♯ E G			
B♭7	B♭ D F A♭			
B7	B D♯ F♯ A			

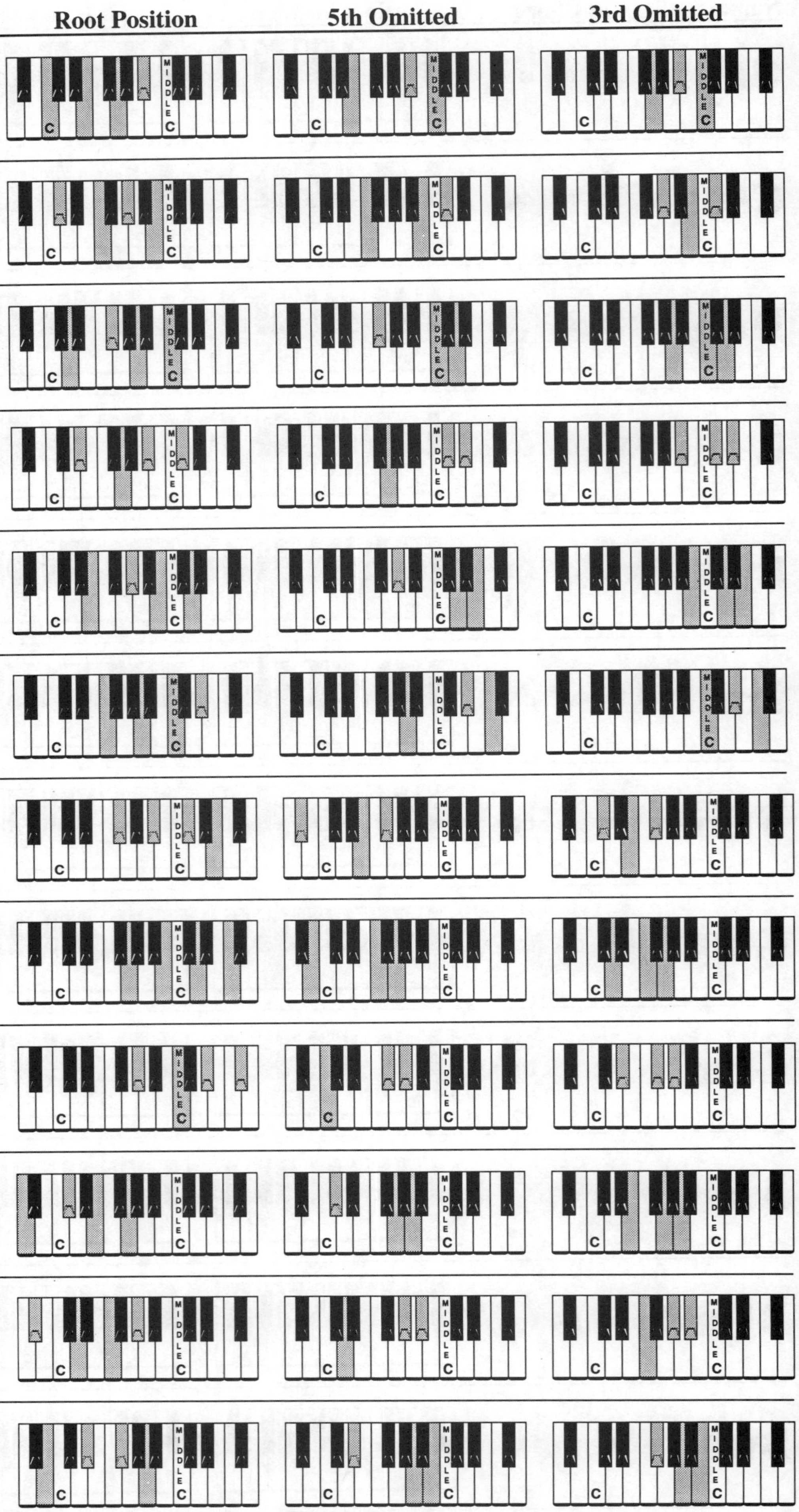

Minor Seventh Chord Chart

Chord Name	Notes In Chord	Root Position	5th Omitted	3rd Omitted
Cm7	C Eb G Bb		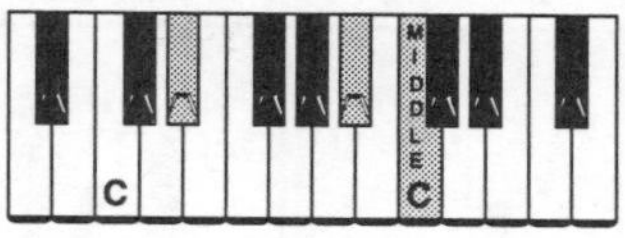	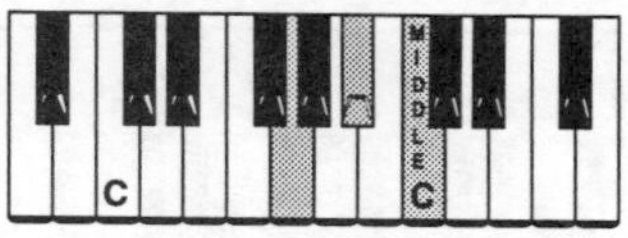
C#m7	C# E G# B			
Dm7	D F A C	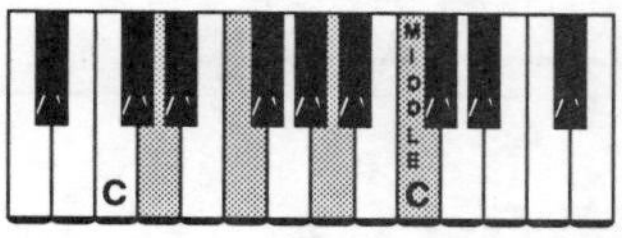		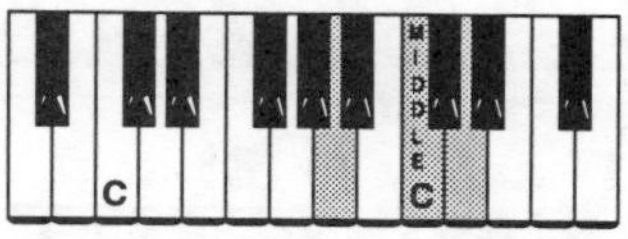
Ebm7	Eb Gb Bb Db			
Em7	E G B D		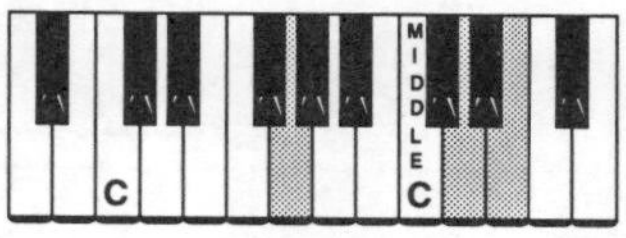	
Fm7	F Ab C Eb			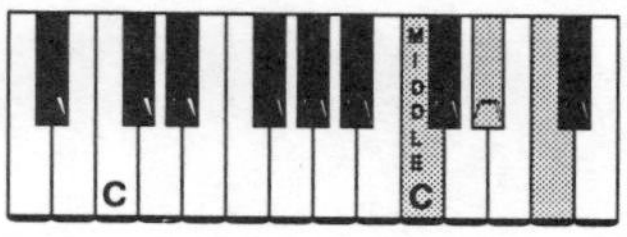
F#m7	F# A C# E	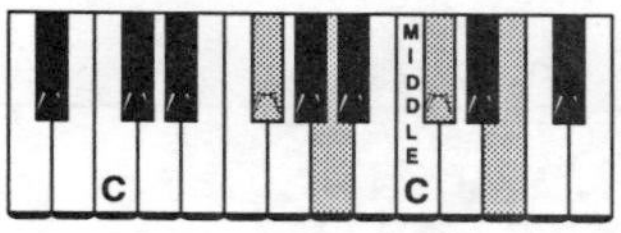		
Gm7	G Bb D F			
G#m7	G# B D# F#			
Am7	A C E G		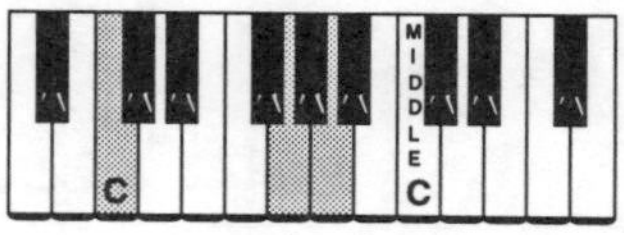	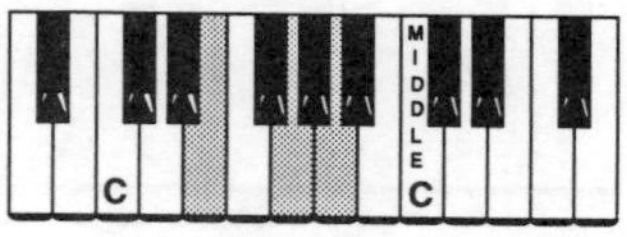
Bbm7	Bb Db F Ab			
Bm7	B D F# A			

Augmented Chord Chart

Chord Name	Notes In Chord	Chord Name	Notes In Chord	Chord Name	Notes In Chord
C aug	C E G♯	C♯ aug	C♯ F A	D aug	D F♯ B♭
E♭ aug	E♭ G B	E aug	E G♯ C	F aug	F A C♯
F♯ aug	F♯ B♭ D	G aug	G B E♭	G♯ aug	G♯ C E
A aug	A C♯ F	B♭ aug	B♭ D F♯	B aug	B E♭ G

Diminished Chord Chart

Chord Name	Notes In Chord	Chord Name	Notes In Chord	Chord Name	Notes In Chord
C dim	C E♭ F♯	C♯ dim	C♯ E G	D dim	D F A♭
E♭ dim	E♭ F♯ A	E dim	E G B♭	F dim	F A♭ B
F♯ dim	F♯ A C	G dim	G B♭ C♯	G♯ dim	G♯ B D
A dim	A C E♭	B♭ dim	B♭ C♯ E	B dim	B D F